Plum Warner's Last Season (1920)

Novels

Timbermills (1938)
The Gold Garland (1939)
Cold Pastoral (1946)
The House of the Living (1947)

Criticism

The Spirit Above the Dust
a study of Herman Melville (1951)

Cricket

Batsman's Paradise (1955)
Jack Hobbs (1960)
Walter Hammond (1962)
Sing All a Green Willow (1967)

SIR PELHAM WARNER

Photo: Radio Times Hulton Picture Library

RONALD MASON

Plum Warner's Last Season (1920)

Then from the dawn it seem'd there came, but faint
As from beyond the limit of the world,
Like the last echo born of a great cry
Sounds, as if some fair city were one voice
Around a king returning from his wars.
—TENNYSON, The Passing of Arthur

LONDON
EPWORTH PRESS

IN MEMORIAM
GREVILLE STEVENS
QUEM HONORIS CAUSA NOMINO

Contents

Contents

vii

Preface and Acknowledgements

As always, I have been sustained throughout the preparation of this book by active help and ready generosity; I hope very much that my thanks and acknowledgements will not sound perfunctory, for I am most grateful for it all. First I would like to thank Mr. Stephen Green, the MCC's curator, for his assistance most courteously given, and likewise Mr. Peter Ellis, the librarian of the Cricket Society, for the loan of necessary books. My friends Tom Evans and Duggie Dalziel, who have been here before, entrusted me with valuable *Wisdens* and concealed the weary resignation that they must have felt. My son Nick put himself out considerably in aid of my search for photographs; my wife put herself out considerably, full stop. I think they know how grateful I am, but that must not prevent me from saying so again, here and now. Mr. G. D. Martineau and Mr. Leslie Frewin kindly gave me permission to use the quotation on page 16, and I have seen that formal credit is given, on the captions, to the various agencies owning the copyrights of the photographs reproduced. To all these I would like to say thank you.

The books I used were few but select; the relevant *Wisdens*,

Warner's *My Cricketing Life*, Jack Hobbs' *My Cricket Memories*,
little more. Three articles published this year in *The Cricketer*,
to whose Editor I am indebted for an early sight of certain
of the proofs, gave me some valuable supplementary material.
One of these was by Alec Waugh, the other two by Greville
Stevens, no less.

The name of Greville Stevens brings me up short. Without
him there might not have been this victorious story to tell
at all, so integral a part did his nineteen-year-old self play in
the sequence of matches that I have taken it upon myself to
chronicle; without his more recent personal encouragement,
advice, and I think I can say approval, the colour and detail
of this book might have been even more meagre than they
are. From the moment I approached him he was, with no
reservation at all, enthusiastically helpful; he wrote me letter
after letter, searched out and entrusted me with private scrap-
books and records, read most of the manuscript, corrected and
suggested, identified himself in the friendliest way with the
enterprise. Sadly, he was not to see it finished; the chapter on
the last great match, which I had been so anxious for him to
see and approve, was not yet in type when the news of his
sudden illness, followed soon after by that of his death, took
much of the savour out of the whole venture. He had survived
by nearly a month the fiftieth anniversary of that last triumphant contest; and his last public utterance had been the fine
tribute in the *Cricketer* article to Plum's memory. I cherish
for my own part this generous and salty personality who did
me so much kindness, and who retained up to the very last
the spirited lively graces of the gifted young man whom Plum
so wisely and so fortunately fostered. I have dedicated what I
hope is a happy book to Greville Stevens' happy memory;
I wish I could have handed it over to the man himself.

RONALD MASON

Banstead
October 1970

1) *The Theme*

EVERY now and then Fact goes one better than Fiction, and demands acceptance as if it were just a good story told to excite or to amuse. It serves in this disillusioned world the very salutary purpose of silencing the sceptic, who in these wicked days since the fall of Man so often enjoys the satisfaction of the last destructive word. Every now and then the truth confounds him. Happily the sceptic is sometimes a sportsman; more happily still, he is occasionally a cricketer; and when the cricketer-sceptic is confounded he has the grace to enjoy his own confusion.

For the cricketer cannot be a sceptic all the time; of necessity his addiction tends to make him a romantic. The game itself is too firmly founded in visual beauty and felicity of conception, and too traditionally inseparable from the perennial national clichés of white-clad figures patterned on green grass and surrounded with historic rural community emblems, ever to be entirely dissociated from moods of nostalgia or contentment which may not be proof against the cooler ironies but at least provide occasional and necessary refuge.

The cricketer builds patterns of activity and of memory out of his association with the game, and these, though removed from any apparent relevance to problems of any importance, exist for him in a world of crisis and conflict apart from our own world but akin to it, and exact from player and spectator alike considerable tolls of emotion and allegiance. And it comes about that cricket matches, artificial romantic dramas of no significance whatever, can, if the player or spectator or the reader has absorbed himself into the tradition, be as compulsive in the memory, as productive of genuine imaginative response, as any historic event or work of art can be. Before this experience the sceptic is, for the moment, put to silence. He may wish that it did not happen, but he cannot deny that it does. Cricket, like international and social movements, has a vivid history, as full of character and crisis as its more important counterpart.

It is a blend of these two elements that is my concern in this book; and it is pleasant to think that when we have followed once again, and in detail this time, this celebrated series of matches that took place half a century ago and because of the course that they took and the personalities who were at their centre have never been forgotten, even by many who never saw them, we may discover in our search that the apparent detachment between the arbitrary patterns of a game on the one hand and the insistent relevance of real experience on the other is not so real as the sceptic would have us believe.

It is rather an odd task that I have set myself; for I am writing for two sets of readers, barely compatible with each other. For what I am hoping to do is to present the story of Plum Warner's last season, both to those who, in a manner of speaking, know all about it already, and to those who do not. The first group don't need to be introduced to the topic – 'Oh, yes, of course, Plum Warner's last season, very good, very good, we know all about that, good luck', is a fair representation of their response. As for the others it is much more likely to be – 'Plum

Warner, who's he?' Knowledge on the one hand, indifference on the other; am I beating my head against a double brick wall?

Let me address the second group first. I have told them little already but that Fact has outbid Fiction here; let me provide a more expressive outline. Fifty years ago is the time; the hero a popular and dedicated cricketer, for many years captain and chief personality of his county, now in his late forties and playing, as already announced, his last season of first-class cricket. The war is over and cricket is alive again; and the massive spectator-interest, sharpened but not satisfied by the first experimental post-war season of 1919, and keenly responsive to the re-introduction of the full three-day game in 1920, is unencumbered by any diversionary touring team from overseas.

Focus is therefore held steady on the county Championship; and our hero's county, never a favourite, is at the end of July nine or ten places down and barely considered as an outside bet. Interest and sympathy concentrate more specifically upon the hero himself; his own performances, modest and unspectacular, divert attention from the mounting success that his side encounters in the first few days of August. Match after match is won, certain of them by cliff-hanger margins; throughout August tension builds up. No less than eight wins are clocked up in a row; and at the very last it is calculated that this dangerously delayed spurt can get them to the final pinnacle *if*, and only *if*, they win their last match outright; and this last match, played at Lord's in a seething atmosphere of tingling excitement, remains largely their opponent's game until half-way through the last crowded day. The heat stays on; there is no single isolatable moment when fortune can be seen to swing to our man's side; but swing it does, the balance tilts, the forces of right prevail, the hero's end is a glorious crowning on his home ground among his lifelong friends. Fact has done better than Fiction; only a very gullible schoolboy would have believed this sequence of improbabilities if he had read them in the *Boy's Own Paper*.

And yet, I insist, still addressing my friends of the second group, it could, and I hope does, make a terrific story. As detailed above it is corny enough in all conscience; but there is so much more to be taken into account. There is Plum Warner's unusual personality: for example, his simplicity, his gentleness, his strange schoolboyish immersion at the age of nearly fifty in every relevant and irrelevant detail of this game; his power to attract love and loyalty; his quaint, stiff, upright, blinkered, old-world public school tradition of behaviour and assumption that invested this pastime with a kind of fervid moral purpose yet left his charm and simplicity radiant and unencumbered – all the disparate elements and individuals in his team were resolved in the unity of loyalty into one of the most powerful elevens in Championship history. There were the fascinating and vital characters and talents of the team itself. There was all that and more beside; there were the varied opponents, cavalier and hospitable like Somerset and Hampshire, craggily formidable like Yorkshire, dangerous like Surrey with genius and promise and intelligence. There was the weather. There was the large and eager public. There was the holiday season. There was the pervasive, lovely, life-enhancing sense of grateful liberation from the deadly immediacy of war.

All these factors, combined with courage and humour and luck and a fortunate variety of skills, lifted Plum Warner and his team and his last season and his last match clean out of the regions of the commonplace and fairly into the areas of epic. Epic is the word, I think, provided that we keep our heads and remember that we are admittedly in a miniscule context. Call it epic, not drama; there are few basic conflicts here, no divisions of mind, no comic or tragic implications; but there is an element of Odyssean homecoming. Odysseus came to Ithaca after many changes and chances of fortune; Plum Warner

came to his Championship honours in the last over of his last
match after a series of variegated struggles that it must have
been even more tense and testing to live through than to read
about – and that is saying a lot.

So much for the uninitiates, my second group, to whom I
have been trying to sell this theme. But the message should
perhaps suffice too for those whose impression was that they
knew all about it already. It is, like other *loci classici* in cricket
history, a commonplace moment enough; but what set of
events, solidified as a commonplace in the public's, or even the
addict's, mind, cannot do from time to time with a re-
examination? If it doesn't clarify anything that we knew before,
it may at the very least re-create more vividly and immediately
for cricket-lovers an experience most memorably rich in
enjoyment and in skill. And it may re-create, too, some of the
characters who are vitally important ingredients in the
narrative.

For not all cricket-lovers remember everybody, and many
of these names, even those who were in their own day great
household names, will have to have some of their original
authority restored. Do Hearne or Mann or Durston mean as
much even to enthusiasts to-day as they did fifty years ago?
I doubt it; it is up to me to re-establish them. And my faith in
the memories even of dedicated schoolboys wavered badly when
on a day only shortly after the Second World War I caught
sight of Patsy Hendren in the crowd at a match at Hastings
and was rewarded (when I pointed him out to a bunch of
eager chattering lads in school caps) with the innocent question
'Who's Patsy Hendren?' Are those boys, now rising thirty,
having to explain to their nearest and dearest who Denis
Compton was or Peter May? It is part of the duty of the cricket-
lover, and even more so of the cricket-lover with scribbler's
itch, to keep green the memory of those who helped to mould
the cricket-loving corner of his life.

Sitting in that corner, like the celebrated Jack in the rhyme,

I have pulled out a Plum. Concentrating on him for a while may help us all to understand how personality no less than outstanding skill can affect the course and the living image of this beautiful and complex game, and how the modest private triumph of one good cricketer who was perhaps not a great one became as personal to all cricket-lovers as if Plum's pleasure had been their own, and can still transmit, after fifty years of ruin and revolution at all levels, a more electrifying message of pleasure and of pride than half a hundred of more illustrious achievements that take up wider spaces in the record-books.

2) *The Man*

WITHOUT the man himself this story would lose character
and purpose; so much of the tension is centred about this frail
but tenacious individual that it would be absurd to try to
describe it without making his figure distinctive.

The name of Plum Warner, common coin in cricket gossip
fifty years ago, is less so now. For very many years he held a
quite unusual position of celebrity and authority in the game,
a tribute even more to his personality than to the quality of his
cricket, admirable though that was – a character who seemed
to carry for much of his career the weight and responsibility
of an administrator as much as a player, an elder statesman at
the age when by many people in the lost territories outside
Lord's and the Oval he would have been voted as still a young
man. He was so natural a leader that especially towards the end
of his career, when his physical appearance was such that it
seemed that any light breeze coming in over mid-off from the
Nursery End would have blown him away, one was surprised
that he was, in fact, so good a cricketer; it needed memory and
intelligence to realize that in fact he had been formidably good
at the game all his life.

Yet the fact that he was a natural leader did not obtrude as it has been known to do in others; he was no presumptuous parade-ground martinet. He leavened his authority with a winning humility, a grace not given to many but given to Plum Warner in plenty. A considerable personality – yet not too considerable to attract the common affections. Part of his popularity, I am convinced, derived from an inescapable illusion that he needed to be cherished and protected. There was a vulnerability about him that the crowd honoured and loved while they identified with it. Other great captains who lacked this – MacLaren, Jardine, Armstrong, Bradman, I pick names at random – were loved less. This is not the whole truth about Warner's popularity, but it is an essential part of it – just as his popularity is not the whole truth about his success and its shining culmination that is now our concern, but is an essential part of its enduring effect. But to come back and look at the man, that is the necessary thing.

Pelham Francis Warner, to give him for the first and last time the full names he was entitled to, was the product in many senses of an older age than ours. To-day he would look perhaps like a little of an anachronism. And, even to his own family, he would seem to have trailed his initial clouds of glory for an unusually long distance, since, at his birth in 1873, he was the youngest of the eighteen children of a brilliant and celebrated Attorney-General of Trinidad who was nearly sixty-eight when his son was born – and who was actually just two days old himself on the date of the Battle of Trafalgar.

From 1873 to 1887, when his father died and the family moved to England, the boy enjoyed what sounds like the typically cushioned and comfortable existence of a colonial administrator's household; and there, it is to be presumed, picked up for better or for worse the values and the assumptions that did him duty for the rest of his life. Gentle, courteous, unexacting, waited on and bowled to by the natives, the family and its members reclined unquestioningly upon the upper crust, the one with jam on; gardens, swimming-pools, pet ponies, dances in the great ballroom when the Fleet was in, the *Field* and the *Illustrated London News* on the library table; the elegant quiet boy in the elegant privileged surroundings prepared himself happily for his strange special career and his strange special fame.

He took his unassuming talents and charm through the brashness of post-Arnold Rugby and the enviable cloistered hush of pre-Nuffield Oxford, and was schooled without friction or disillusion into an almost inevitable place of honour among the illustrious sporting coteries of Edwardian England. A consuming love of cricket, fostered from birth among the palm trees and cherished into intensity in a gravely-dedicated nature, saw him to a proficiency which was partly of course a gift of the gods but also without doubt a disciplined creation of his own addiction. He knew all about Lord's before he ever saw it; once he had seen it he loved it like a secret place in his own heart; before he left it for the last time several generations later he had virtually re-injected it with the breath of his own mild but distinctive personality. If the great ground enshrines the memory of any single man to-day, in the way, say, that the Oval is still pervaded by the essential presence of Jack Hobbs (and it is easy to see what enormous competition there is) it enshrines this man's, and his virtues and his traditions too.

Plum Warner – he got his nickname at Rugby and nobody ever thought of him thereafter as anything else – had acquired his love of cricket before he ever settled in England, but it was Rugby and Tom Emmett's coaching there that set him for life in this abiding obsession. We who love the game too, no less devotedly we hope but perhaps less exclusively, must often, while contemplating this career of his, put a curb on a natural stirring of sheer envy at the good fortune of a man whom circumstances allowed, nay encouraged, to pursue fully and enjoyably the game of his enduring delight as player, spectator, journalist, selector and lawgiver for seventy-five years with barely a break for meals. It truly does seem, as we look back

at his long life, that in the course of it all his gifts, all his considerable intelligence, perseverance, imagination, and scholarship were channelled single-mindedly away from the other
more central preoccupations of life into this one pursuit. I had
said emotions and sympathies too, but there it is quite clear
from the accounts of everyone who knew him that there were
no bounds whatever to his considerate kindliness and delicacy.
If ever a life was devoted to a game, his was. That he had the
enlarging leisure was his good luck; he concentrated as closely
and conscientiously upon his passionate pastime as if it were a
life's intense vocation – as, in a manner, it was.

He read law at Oxford, he wrote fluently and not ungrace-
fully (on cricket, of course) for the Press. The law I imagine
he forgot as soon as he had sat the papers; he never forgot a
single fact about cricket law, theory, or history. He was
happiest actually playing; he was nearly fifty before he gave
up the first-class game, and he certainly went on at a lower
level for more than a dozen years longer. For the rest he was
fulfilled best when watching, or describing, or advising, or
administering, or remembering it all. His single-minded
dedication, utterly serious and yet not refusing to admit
humour, shone out of him like a light.

As a young man of twenty-one he associated closely for the
first time with the cream of the Middlesex amateurship of the
heyday. First-class cricket up to 1914, and possibly even a little
later, was a fine standing advertisement for the social-political
idea of the Two Nations, and no better epitome of its spirit
could be found than the great metropolitan country of
Middlesex, centrally established in the awesome seat of high
authority at Lord's.

To the latter-day eye the team is redolent of all the languid
handsome graces of the leisured classes of that opulent age, all
bright blazers and dilettantism; unworried, generous, frequenters of clubland, country-house weekends, regimental messes,
champagne supper-parties, the world of Lady Windermere,

losing her fan at almost this very instant of time at the glittering St. James' Theatre; assisted in the good work by a small handful of bronzed deferential underpaid professionals with heavy moustaches, who at Lord's came, went, changed clothes and for all one knows were permitted to feed and sleep, in a humble rabbit-hutch fifty yards away from the main pavilion. Not that the amateurs were particularly dilettante about their cricket; they were, when Warner joined them, a regal gathering – Sir Timothy O'Brien, Gregor MacGregor, the brilliant and prolific Stoddart and the captain A. J. Webbe, all resounding names evocative of the enormous skills and talents that the history of cricket is so rich in. They worked at their game as vigorously as their hardy professionals Jack Hearne and Rawlin, and, on the field, never did other than acknowledge them as equals or, when appropriate, betters. And what impinged most upon the young Warner when he joined them, a ready recipient for it, was their innate and infectious courtesy. Warner, a shy man, never for the rest of his life forgot Webbe's welcome to him when he first entered the room, rising at once to greet the stranger and make him feel at home. Warner said, years after his own retirement, that in later times when he became captain he always, when a new man came to play, had in mind the way Webbe first met him. Generations of Middlesex players will be able to bear this out. The generous goodwill that went along with the easy living was strengthened in Warner into a life-principle of sympathy and respect, reinforcing his natural charm to mature the personality whom the public of 1920 were to honour so happily with their acclamation and their affection.

Before he was twenty-seven he had toured half the globe; teams travelled in those days with less publicity and panache and often to unexpected places. The West Indies, Portugal, America (twice, if you can believe it) and Canada were all happily and briefly invaded, and by now he was even being captain; and South Africa was added to his traveller's bag before the nineteenth century was out. Moreover, an unofficial tour which he led to New Zealand and Australia a year or two later led indirectly to the MCC taking over for the first time the responsibility for the next Australian trip; and Warner, not without a certain amount of opposition from angry MacLaren supporters, led the first MCC team to Australia with huge enjoyment, confounding the malicious prophets who prognosticated complete defeat by winning the rubber 3–2.

By now he was thirty and a fully-matured player. In a fine glossy compilation of 1899 or 1900 called *The Book of Cricket*, edited by C. B. Fry and published by George Newnes Ltd., gilt-edged coffee-table size and weighing about half a stone, he is elegantly pictured in a series of beautiful photographs, slim, neatly-tailored and grave, wearing an O.U.C.C. cap, with the dews of youth still upon him and a courtly deference in his every pose. 'He represents', says the text, which in divers places bears the sign-manual of the irrepressible editor himself, 'the best kind of public-school player . . . his orthodoxy is of the kind that appears natural, such is the ease that much practice gives . . . Warner has made all that is artificial in batting quite his own'. (What an unusually shrewd observer was Fry – thus early to note not only the diligence that with Warner turned a fair player into a very good one but also the art which in Warner concealed the drudgery of that diligence and turned it to the advantage of his play.)

A classical batsman, is the general summing-up; though it was noted, and this was less orthodox in 1900 than it would be to-day, that he got a large number of his runs on the leg side – 'he is a very determined player on the leg-stump' (Fry 1900), interestingly corroborated by a later spectator – 'he spent the whole bloody day tickling singles off his legs' (a friend of mine who saw an innings of his in 1910, recounting it to me in the nineteen-fifties). 'A passable bowler at country-houses' (ah, the sunlight on the lawns, the servants moving among the guests with champagne, the band playing) 'and' (here in his twenty-seventh year, his character is formed for life) 'a golden treasury of all that ever happened, or was likely to happen, in the game of cricket'. Fry has here caught the compulsive encyclopaedist, early and entire.

Between 1903 and 1912 Warner played in fifteen Test Matches. It was an age of supreme batsmen and it is not perhaps surprising that with Fry, Ranji, Hayward, Hobbs, Rhodes, Tyldesley, MacLaren, Spooner and Jackson among the competitors he never commanded a regular place. In fact he only played twice against Australia in England in the whole of his career; and somehow it is not as a Test cricketer that we tend to remember him, though there should be no doubt at all that he was of Test metal. For most spectators and for all of us who never saw him play but remember him as an essential part of the background of cricket history, his playing days are identified with Middlesex; even more intimately still, with Lord's. His later years as commentator, adviser, statesman in this little world, merely fill out the image and give it lustre and depth; for the watchers in 1920 who caught their breath during his last great sequence of matches, it was Plum Warner of Middlesex whose crises and epic adventures kindled their sympathy and delight – Plum Warner of Middlesex, slim and slight among his formidable juniors, wearing his Harlequin cap.

This Harlequin cap he of course appropriated as his emblem, and the association will always remain. It is another odd symbol of his times; there is a curious connection between this rather flamboyant emblem of exclusive honour and the inevitable passing of an age. The only persons entitled to wear it are Oxford Blues, plus a very few additional invitees of the current University captain; it has bizarre and vivid quarterings in blue, maroon and buff, and generations of Oxford cricketers have paraded it proudly like a banner. In the nineties, and indeed up to the nineteen twenties, cricket photographs are vivid with it; it was worn almost as a matter of course by old Blues when they played for their counties; and in the days before the England cap and sweater were regulation uniform when England took the field, it did not seem out of place in Tests. I think that I am right in saying that Douglas Jardine was the last England captain to sport it in a Test series, and that his defiant wearing of it in the 1932–33 bodyline matches in Australia added marginally to the rifts of misunderstanding and distrust with which that unfortunate tour was bedevilled. Nowadays it is virtually never seen at all on the first-class field; a social philosopher could write a thesis on this minor sartorial curiosity. In the nineties and early nineteen hundreds, Warner was one of a crowd wearing it, yet because as he grew older he never wore any other, and because in a manner it seemed in its histrionic gaiety to accentuate the unfading quality of his youthful enthusiasm, Plum and his Harlequin cap became inseparable emblems in the public's admiration. It meant little enough, I suppose; but it stood for a kind of distinction, a sort of honour in which the fortunate wearer might take a modest and exclusive pride, that is now all but departed. If there is any one element in Warner's image that represented something that was of his age, and perhaps class, that is less valid now than it was then, it is perhaps best epitomized in the Harlequin cap. He would have performed just as well without it; but it was an essential part of him as his admirers knew him, and nobody would wish it away. The colours faded easily and quickly; he did not.

Indeed he did not; he must have been, constitutionally, as tough as an old boot. When he was young he looked frail and tenuous, when he was older he looked frail and transparent; his career, and his life after his career ended, were punctuated with enervating and sometimes desperate illnesses. His years at Rugby were bedevilled by the effects of an operation, in his first two seasons at Oxford repeated bouts of influenza ruined his chances of a Blue, and time and again in later life severe duodenal attacks savaged him without warning. For an appreciable spell at one period he was visited with griping pains at 11.30 a.m. and 4.30 p.m. with precise regularity, as if in the power of some diabolical clock. For several matches in the 1909 season he was compelled to rest from cricket altogether; he was, it will be remembered, dangerously and spectacularly struck down, after the first match of the great Australian tour of 1911–12, by a violent internal attack from which his recovery was very slow – yet he was playing in Tests the next summer, not very effectively, but he was there. His hardworking War service in Whitehall was interrupted twice by serious illness; and he suffered at least two severe bouts in the nineteen-twenties, which culminated in an operation which seems to have done the trick that had eluded his medical advisers over so many and frustrating and weary years, for he was never so fiercely assailed again. But from one end of his active life to the other Warner rode storms of illness as Odysseus weathered the thunderbolts of Poseidon. Lesser men would have had remark-ably valid excuses for dying five or six times over; Plum Warner lived to be eighty-nine. Poseidon could never sink this particular raft, at any rate until long after the epic journey was over.

The Harlequin cap gave him the appearance of a chubby boy; the successive illnesses lent him the aspect of an ailing parent. In whatever *persona* he was accepted by his crowds of followers and admirers, and a blend of both was in his common mien, it meant that they felt towards him a cherishing protectiveness. They saw, they could not help seeing, his vulnerability; they saw, they could not help seeing, the vivid courage with which he faced out these private battles of his. He aged: his face wrinkled; when he took off his Harlequin cap he was grey and bald – yet his slim light figure kept its lines, he preserved a lissom boyish quality in his movements just as to the very end of his life there were quarters of his mind that (with the gains and the losses that this entails) had not progressed far beyond the sixth-form room at Rugby. His crowds of admirers looked for him so and loved him and approved him so; there have not been many cricketers who have so solidly and permanently endeared themselves to so many people without the blessings of brilliance, eccentricity or spectacular habits or attainments. Plum Warner's play, like Plum Warner's character, was neither brilliant, eccentric nor spectacular. He was quiet, thoughtful, orthodox, a little cramped, conscientious. You felt that he batted with knitted brows; he spent the whole bloody day, as my friend said, tickling singles off his legs. This muted and ailing Establishmentarian is not the usual mould of hero to which the common man in his thousands gives his heart, yet the common spectator in his thousands all over the cricket-playing globe offered his heart to Plum.

Yet it would be quite wrong even to hint that he was less of a player than a character. There is no doubt at all that for the many years of his temperate prime he was a very considerable batsman indeed. After all, he made nearly 30,000 runs, and his career average was not far off 40; he made 60 centuries, more than Arthur Shrewsbury ever made, or Wilfred Rhodes, or Fishlock or Hallows or Fagg or MacLaren; he was for a dozen years or more one of the most dependable opening batsmen of the country, watching the shine off all the leading bowlers from Barnes to Bill Hitch with the unvarying scholarly concentration entirely typical of his committed life. G. D. Martineau, one of the few poets of cricket to whom it has been granted to rise above doggerel, has hit off beautifully and evocatively the redolent memory of the crowded legendary days before 1914 in a most expressive quatrain more than fitted to my purpose:

> Hard-benched, straw-hatted, glad, ingenuous crowds –
> Bold rhymes declaimed, that only Craig could sell –
> Blythe bowling like a dance of summer clouds –
> And P. F. Warner mastering the spell . . .

Anybody, and Plum could do it, who could bring the resources of a trained mind to master – and the apt exact word is 'master' – the wizardry of that beautiful and deadly bowler is an artist to be honoured for his artistry. In that haunting quatrain the essence not only of an age, but of a great character and talent, is magically entrapped.

It has not been my purpose, in preparing this picture of him, to chronicle in detail the progress of his scores and his career. This chapter is designedly impressionistic rather than bio-graphical. In order to take some reminiscent part in the excitement of his last season, it is necessary to have before us the image of this man as the watchers in 1920 had it before them. No doubt some of the more fanatical sort had his records at their finger-tips, but the majority, surely, accepted him readily as they found him and watched him at Lord's, carrying in their minds the awareness that here was a much-tried but perennially-active veteran with a generation of cricket experience behind him; who had captained England in many Tests; who had carried cricket on the seven seas to more parts of the habitable globe than most of them could count; who had led Middlesex into the field for as long as most of them could remember; who in the destroying preoccupations of war had still kept the game alive at Lord's in the intervals of his own duties and his own sicknesses, and was now in the re-awakening seasons of 1919 and 1920 strongly representative of a resilience of spirit which communicated itself to the severely-tried multitudes and refreshed them.

He wasn't all that young, he wasn't all that well, he had been battered as they all, by 1919, felt that they had been; yet he was bright as a button, wearing his Harlequin cap in the sunshine, reappearing from behind the destructive veils and reminding them of some lost innocence that was not beyond being found again. This in part, I believe, was the secret of the peculiar popularity of Plum Warner in the earliest moments of the post-war years. He sounded a note of regeneration and hope; everything would be as it was again. We could thankfully go on from where we reluctantly left off.

3) *The Team*

YET it was not as simple as it looked; the man Warner, knowing himself to be neither young nor strong, must really be regarded as extremely lucky to have been fit enough to continue first-class cricket at all after the War, and it was only the vivid youthful flame inside him that sustained him to the physical effort; but this stirring story, though naturally it has in Warner the individual its origin and its centre, is dependent for its progress on innumerable other factors of great complexity.

If Warner was to triumph, and nobody, least of all himself, could have systematically planned this, he had to have with him a collection of ten or more associates the sum of whose unanimity was somehow greater than all their individual talents. He had to have a winning team, and he had to make it up out of the ingredients available. He hadn't only to keep his own form and fitness, but he had to make sure that everyone else in the side did too. Sides don't often win Championships on a few personal successes alone; it needs a season's back-breaking perseverance by round about a dozen people at least not only willing their best but being permitted by Providence to do it and succeed with it oftener than be baulked. Middlesex in the spring of 1920 would hardly have given you sixpence for their chances. I doubt if they gave the idea of Championship honours much serious thought until the last miraculous month began to light sparks of excitement and anticipation in them, jointly and severally. Under the surface of the bare accounts of the matches in *Wisden*, even between the lines of the score-sheets themselves, you can feel the belated but compulsive tension rising as the days of August tick off one after the other. The team found its unity and its strength as it went along; they grew up in it from within, inspired and fostered partly by the personality of Warner himself, but derived directly, of course, from the immense talent and adaptability of each individual.

Middlesex had no great reason to complain of War losses, at least in the usual sense of disability or death. The one great gap was the departure for his homeland of the brilliant and reliable all-rounder Frank Tarrant, who with young Jack Hearne in 1914 had constituted perhaps the most attractive and successful pair of all-rounders in the country, making between them in that doomed sunshiny season just under 4,000 runs and taking nearly 250 wickets. For the moment we will not worry about the runs; Middlesex have very rarely found diffi-culty in collecting them from somewhere or other; but wickets are rather more important commodities, since if you are to win a match you are normally required to capture twenty, and in 1919 Tarrant was back in Australia trading in racehorses (which I suppose he enjoyed more than playing first-class cricket, though unless you concentrate only on the purely financial side of it I cannot imagine why) and Hearne was troubled by an injury to a finger and hardly bowled at all. The bowling in fact was in a very dubious state indeed and nobody in Middlesex felt in the least bit sanguine about it. The team was, as regularly it had been before the War, powerfully stocked with amateurs. It was just as Plum had found it on the day when A. J. Webbe rose so charmingly to greet him; he himself now did the honours with his own gentle grace, and round him thronged the dashing and prolific figures who just before the war had adorned the Lord's Schools fortnight or the Eton and Harrow match or the University game itself – names like F. T. Mann, R. H. Twining, Nigel Haig, G. E. V. Crutchley, the Hon. C. N. Bruce (Eton, Harrow, Winchester preponderate in this list) and a dozen others only a little less proficient.

This new generation of Middlesex amateurs are perhaps just that little less languid and privileged than their seniors of Warner's earlier years. In those times the Middlesex side posed for its photograph looks uneasily like a random selection from the Cavalry Club (the amateurs with their trimmed assertive moustaches) and a grocer's half-day at the seaside (the professionals with their bushy plebeian ditto). The immediately post-war collection of amateurs seemed, not unnaturally, a little leaner and less leisured than their forerunners, and although nobody is going to deny that they were a very able bunch of cricketers indeed, we are now clearly in at the beginning of the expansion of the professional core of the county. As a general rule this was bound to make for valuable consolidation; there was in its earlier stages a perceptible tendency to admit an amateur when he felt like playing, rather than when he was indisputably better than anyone else available. From now on this applies less and less.

There was something a little odd about the 1919 season. The players drew in deep breaths of free air, the spectators relaxed in joy and satisfying numbers, the weather for the most part shed all the warmth and light upon the revelry that could be desired – but a sense of dissatisfaction remains. This seems to be largely due to the experimental substitution of two-day for three-day cricket as the basis for the Championship fixtures. The number of days was cut down but the tally of hours was correspondingly extended, which meant that the day's play went on until 7.30, and days in the field were long days indeed. The fact that the eager spectatorship developed the habit of getting up and going home to supper just as the game was getting exciting did not seriously bother the players, or at least rated as a minor inconvenience only; but by half-way through the summer a leg-weary lassitude began to invade the regular players, and it was clear to everyone that the quality of the cricket was suffering.

Warner himself said that well before the end of the season he was a dead dog (he had an engaging habit of zoologizing himself; in his old age he would often refer to himself as a 'delicate old dog', and I remember it being reported that when some newspaper contacted him on what was to be his very last birthday of all he expressed surprise and pleasure that anyone should wish to hear about 'an old bird' like him); he also, more objectively, commented disapprovingly that too many inferior batsmen made large scores that season against bowlers and fielders who were physically exhausted. Middlesex being, as already noted, conspicuously short on bowlers that year, suffered presumably from leg-weariness and late-night blues rather more than other counties more fortunately endowed, but I am quite sure that Warner would have made the same complaint even if they had won the Championship, which there was no likelihood of them doing. An entirely unassailable fair-mindedness and generosity were shining Warner characteristics; making up two of the reasons at least why everybody, even his keenest opponents, felt and expressed such deep spontaneous pleasure when he moved to his final triumph.

The 1919 season was, as I have said, odd and experimental; a fresh start that managed to look a little like a false start. Its failure gave the season of 1920, when the status of the three-day game was firmly restored to everyone's relief, the air of a gala celebration when we could thankfully banish all war-time substitutes and taste mother's jam again. There is no doubt that the oddity of the 1919 arrangements, which may seem sublimely irrelevant to the matches fought out at Lord's in the August of

1920, contributed by their air of unreality to the additional smack of excitement and tension which characterized the little epic for which this narrative is preparing. Nevertheless, before we flush the 1919 season down the drains in contempt, it is essential to remind ourselves that if it didn't do anything else it gave the cricketers admirable batting and bowling practice, and that as far as Middlesex is concerned it was invaluable in laying down in indestructible stone the formidable foundation of a great batting side. By the beginning of the 1920 season the Middlesex batting had formed itself into an obstructive and destructive combination of horrifying proficiency, in which experience, determination, elegance and brutally murderous aggression were nicely and effectively blended. I do not think that there can be a better introduction to the story of Warner's year of mounting success than a close and individual inspection of the batsmen-in-chief. I know, and I have already said it not many pages ago, that it is the bowlers who win Championships for counties; nothing that I am going to say will contradict this. But in the purposeful building of this great Middlesex Championship side the batsmen were there first and matured first and we are going to look at them first. The bowlers were there all right, they had to be, but they came later. We shall see them come; it is part of the story.

For years before the War, the Middlesex batting had been opened as of right by Plum Warner himself. This was not a hard-and-fast rule, and he seems to have been adaptably ready to go in anywhere; but there is no doubt that by 1914 he was one of the most experienced and reliable openers in the country. Those intent and absorbed eyes under the knitted conscientious brows had seen the shine off every reputable opening bowler in cricket. Years and years before this there was a certain Gents v. Players match at Lord's in which the great Barnes, opening the bowling for the Players, strained his leg or his back so badly at the end of the first over that he bowled no more during the match. Warner in his comprehensive history

of this fixture, written, I suppose, half a century or so after the
event, comments with a genial mixture of admiration and
pride that that one over was the most testing first over he ever
saw in his career. 'I had to take it', he adds with an amiable
modesty, 'and so I know' – and the spirit quakes before the
thought of an over from Barnes which was even more testing
than any other over from Barnes, and one turns to the score
sheet and observes that it was a maiden, as might have been
expected, and that P. F. Warner made 51, which might easily
have been expected too. A cool and accomplished defender of
the faith against the greatest; this, without implying actual
greatness in himself, is I think an apt enough description of
Warner at his best, who could take anything that came his way
and had the practical ability to survive it. The fact that by 1919
he was beginning to wilt a little in quality is nothing to be
surprised about.

   With Harry Lee, the first in order of going in of the professional batting strength, we are at once in the presence of the
personification of sterling and loyal service coupled with
abilities that were concealed rather than accentuated by his
innate modesty. He was – happily, still is – a short square
amiable Cockney with fair scanting hair and a mild blue eye,
temperate and unassertive, chunky and quizzical. He is to be
seen in contemporary group photographs smiling equably
over the rolls of a turtle-neck sweater, and in some of them
even clutching a pipe. The natural compactness of his movements had not been improved by his War experience, in the
course of which he had been left all night in No Man's Land
with a severe leg wound, and he walked for the rest of a prolonged and popular career with a craggy little limp which he
carried off with adroitness and aplomb. I doubt if even before
his injury his style had been of the free-flowing sort; by now
at any rate it had solidified into a canny and tortured crouch
which made his inconsiderable height less considerable still.
But his blue eyes looked cagily down the wicket out of this

uncomfortable posture and his great muscular adaptability and power saw to it that although defence was his element, the forcing shots went off with every bit as much penetration as if all the classic graces had timed them. As a solid practical opener there were few to equal him in England. By this time he was nearly thirty – the War had cut the heart of his prime right out as it had done for so many others – but he was to voyage on busily and successfully for untold years to come. He was still opening the innings for Middlesex, and getting 100, in 1934; and when you consider that to the ringside's eye view he looked half as old as Time even before Warner gave up, his native indestructibility, communicated always to his batting, can be imagined and accepted.

He was the eldest in a sterling and attractive sequence of brothers; there were two others, one of whom was his junior by fourteen, and the other by seventeen, years – he probably behaved to them like an unusually benevolent grandfather – and in the course of time they both gave great service for years to Somerset, one as a batsman-bowler all-rounder and the other as an unusually capable batsman-wicket-keeper. They were in their several ways less chunky and more lively than their elder brother; but neither was as good a batsman (Harry got into one Test match, they didn't) and neither was so demonstrably hewn out of the living rock. Jack, the middle brother, was unhappily killed in the Second World War; but Frank, the youngest of the Lees, trod Test Match turf for years in later days as one of the most illustrious umpires in the history of cricket. The Lees were, and are, a rare cricketing family, all guts and good-nature; and Harry, trudging cheerfully in by the side of his captain to take up his ugly vigilant crouch, was not only sterling material, but material rich in runs as well.

In Harry Lee we see the journeyman qualities of the typical competent but undistinguished professional batsmen admirably heightened to give the maximum effectiveness. When the first wicket falls and Number Three appears, an altogether different set of standards of appreciation is required. It isn't that this man is better – though, to tell the truth, he is; it is that he is of another sort of order. For this is J. W. Hearne; 'Young Jack' Hearne, so called to distinguish him from his much older cousin Jack, J. T. Hearne, who had sustained the main thrust of Middlesex bowling with immense success for more than twenty years before the War.

Young Jack Hearne is, as I say, a different case; he is not just 'very good', he bears all the marks of undoubted greatness, yet in the long run somehow fails to achieve all that seems to be in his power. To the spectator there was, to the chronicler there still is, a curiously enigmatic quality about him, and it is very difficult to assess exactly what was the reason for this. What his record makes clear, and what everyone who ever played with him continues to insist, is that there was no keener and more self-effacing team-man on the side, and that not only in this year of Warner's triumph but for nearly ten years before and not many short of twenty after he was worth his weight in precious metal to any side he played for. And yet the enigma remains.

He had developed very early indeed, long before the 1914 war, into a young player of immense controlled competence. He had not been coached – he was largely self-taught – but the natural graces of the born stylist came easy to him and he settled very early into a notable elegance and compactness of batmanship as well as reinforcing this remarkable talent by an unusual skill as a highly intelligent leg-spinner with googly very much attached. Rewards came early; he went on tour to Australia before he was twenty-one, and was by no means the least of the successes of that 1911-12 crusade which ended so thick in personal honours. It was at the end of this tour that Warner in a euphoric moment prophesied that in six years he would be the greatest batsman in the world. (I suppose the sage can hardly be blamed for failing to foresee the extraordinary persistence of the genius of Jack Hobbs, who seems in some ways to have been even better after he was forty than he had been before it; but there were other factors that nullified the generous forecast.)

Dizzy heights of attainment aside, there was nothing in 1914 to deny to Jack Hearne the title of by far the most promising all-rounder in English cricket. As already noted, he and Tarrant had carried between them the bulk of the day-to-day burden of Middlesex success; and now the War had ended, he was not yet thirty and the land lay open before him to claim it. His batting had patience, invulnerability, and calm rhythm; his bowling, a neatly-styled economical affair with a smart whippy action and a low deceptive trajectory, expended the minimum of energy and was deceptively venomous. One would have thought that the nineteen-twenties were his for the asking. During that decade he made thousands of runs, took hundreds of wickets, prolonged until far into the thirties his unassuming loyal service – and yet something, I cannot define it, was lacking. He had a delicacy, a curious primness of demeanour that gave his cricket an air of fastidious aloofness. His toes were ever so slightly turned outwards, his cap was set straight on his head, he paced as if on eggs. He had handsome refined ascetic features; if Plum Warner would have passed in Rome as a gentle beneficent cardinal, Jack Hearne could have been a submissive attendant priest. He did not fire the multitudes; what is more, for some inexplicable reason he was almost laughably accident-prone. There were times when it seemed that he only had to put his finger near the ball for it to effect a fracture or a dislocation; again and again he would be missing for weeks together as a result of some mishap or other. Moreover he more than once fell prey to serious illness. This perhaps deepened the lines on his finely-chiselled features, but once he had recovered he always seemed ready to take his accustomed reliable place once more, coolly and dependably deploying his natural classicism, a little sadly and in a muted tone. His greatness resided in his style and his reliability and his philosophy, perhaps, rather than in the fulfilment (for this never quite happened) of his prodigious promise. From the ring of spectators he seemed a slightly aloof, perhaps spinsterish figure; those who knew him speak of his sturdy independence and dry humour, which bodies him out admirably and attractively for those of us who did not. I encountered him once, many years later, when he was for a time coach at my old school; he surprised and in a way delighted me by being much more full-blooded and robust, both in habit and in mind, than he had seemed to me in my youth, and I suppose in his. As an asset to any side short of a world-beating Test XI he has been in the eyes of history under-rated rather than otherwise; that there has to be this slight reservation is perhaps a measure of temperamental or physical failure, but certainly of no inadequacy of technique or spirit.

It is of course true too that he had a reticence of personality that helped in his inevitable overshadowing by his fellow-professional with whom he shared so many prolonged partnerships. He was admittedly unlucky in this: there were not many players who could have remained undimmed in popularity and publicity by the side of this high-pressured crowd-compeller. If Plum Warner resembled a cardinal and Jack Hearne his priest, Patsy Hendren would have made the ideal parishioner of the latter in some remote whitewashed cluster of shebeens on the Connemara coast. He looked like a particularly companionable monkey, with the characteristic long upper lip and humorous pout of the lower that gave you the instant and compulsive impression that he was smoking a white clay pipe with the bowl upside down. Rubbery, lightly-stepping, comical in appearance and behaviour, he radiated a sunny good-humour, played unremittingly but delightfully to the gallery, captivated every Middlesex follower for the best part of thirty years, and became into the bargain one of the three or four most consistently prolific run-scorers of all time.

It is odd to remember that this engaging ball of fire had rather a sputtering start to his cricket career, and for various reasons, War and otherwise, did not establish himself in his rightful place in the county side until he was thirty. As he always behaved like a high-spirited urchin of fifteen, even when he was a year or two off fifty, he became a symbol of perennial life and joy to cricket watchers of all ages, continuing with remarkable zest to score prolifically in first-class cricket until two years before the Second World War, and being active as coach, scorer and even occasionally as player, for years and years after that. He was not an elegant batsman or a stylish one like Hearne; his bottom stuck out provocatively as he awaited the ball, and he was set too low in the water for the easy flowing forward strokes that are the mark of the stylist; but he made up for this by enormous predatory quickness of foot, questing up and down the wicket in twinkling little boots, savaging anything of faulty length with a goloptious rapacity. He had sprung-steel wrists, cut and slashed with fierce power, and was the best hooker in the trade except Jack Hobbs. He ate and drank off fast bowlers, loved them carnivorously like a cannibal – I have never, even forty years later, got over his destruction of the great McDonald at the Oval one day, never – and on fast wickets could score at a tremendous pace. His pugnacious scurrying figure, sleeves rolled only halfway up the forearms, creased cap perked almost anyhow on top of his head, cheerful Irish mouth grinning in generous enjoyment, cannot help but be in everyone's memories of Lord's between the wars. He was a part of the nation's pastoral enjoyment; he even slipped, no doubt without knowing it and indeed mainly for the sake of the rhyme, into a well-known poem by John Betjeman.

He ate and drank off fast bowlers, I said; but I must not blind myself to the fact that for a year or two in his first ventures in Test Matches they made a corresponding meal off him. He wallowed and rioted in runs from 1919 onwards –

but when he faced the Australians in Tests the high flair faltered. Gregory and McDonald in 1921 overturned his jaunty confidence; it took him years of courage and hard work to restore it, in a Test context at least. But once he re-established himself in his own and the selector's eyes, and it was a long up-hill job never perhaps quite convincingly complete, he was tenacious and unwearying and nearly always reliable at an age when most Test players were drawing their pensions. More than once he saved England in 1934, when he was forty-five and his old opponents of the early nineteen-twenties had long been put out to grass. He was a triumph of resilience; it was his odd vulnerability at that crucial time which somehow lowered him from the very topmost company. But he scored more hundreds than anyone has ever done, save Jack Hobbs; and he was a sure prehensile catch and in his early days was as fleet of foot as he was flexible in muscle. Hearne and Hendren, what a pair; Edrich and Compton can match them, but who else?

These were the adamantine core of the batting, and any captain must have felt complacent as he began to pencil down those names. After number four, however, we fall over a bit of a cliff. Not to destruction, I hasten to add, but to a region of talented and random uncertainty, peopled by clubmen and regimental messes, a lucky dip of names to conjure with and names to wonder about, who might or might not be available, who might or might not make a century or take valuable wickets. String off the possibilities and a row of names like E. L. Kidd, H. K. Longman, the Hon. C. N. Bruce, Dr. C. H. Gunasekara and the like pass intermittently before your bemused eyes; all talented and vigorous men, nearly all of them Blues at one time or another, some of them not quite up to it and others a little past it, enjoying their few games of cricket because Plum Warner liked and admired what they were or had been and because they liked and admired what Plum Warner was. The eleven is generally not without a couple of these attractive birds of passage, and some of them cut a very honourable figure in the story to come. They ride into a sort of immortality on the commanding genius and accomplishment of the great professionals, who deferred to them in due order and degree and retired to their rabbit-hutch until required. They were cheerful and adventurous amateurs in the best sense and I have no intention of disparaging their quality. They pulled all the weight they had, and pulled it worthily; that they were of lesser timber than the others was as well-known to them as it is to us. They did what they had to do.

Standing out among the regular amateurs were two future captains of the county, future England players in fact, who matured in stature and quality throughout the time of which I speak and both went well beyond it later. Frank Mann was one, a tall burly ex-Guards Officer who looked it. An expansive personality of great charm, he relied on the scientific disposal of his considerable weight behind a heavily swung bat to bring him a large number of memorable quick-scoring innings. He was a crowd's favourite for this forthright aggressiveness; some years later he had the enormous nerve to hit Wilfred Rhodes, no less, four times on to the roof of the Pavilion at Lord's in the course of a single innings. He became a very popular Middlesex captain, a successful touring captain, and in due time the proud father of another precisely ditto ditto. A straightforward honourable uncomplicated cricketer, he is remembered by all who saw him with unforced pleasure, even by me who saw him hit one of my county's bowlers through the window of my county's Committee Room.

The other was Nigel Haig, a leaner, more active figure altogether, an untiring all-rounder upon whom a great deal of new-ball bowling was to depend for years and years to come. He was a capable and attractive, if never entirely reliable, batsman, an excellent field, an all-round athlete of great reputation in other games beside cricket, and possessed,

I am told, of an agreeably sardonic wit. He could, and some-times did, bowl all day at a brisk fast medium pace off a lovely easy run and free handsome action, varying his pace and flight little but occasionally making the odd one move away or back quite unexpectedly. (More than once he bowled Hobbs with the one that left the pitch late and lifted to take the off bail; he had that kind of dangerous unpredictability.) He survived trimly and youthfully until he was nearly eighty, having captained the county until he was nearly fifty; enlivening what I suppose must be called his old age by playing golf of a very high quality indeed, writing the history of Middlesex cricket, and compiling short and witty biographies for E. W. Swanton's *World of Cricket*. Mann and Haig, the two amateur lieutenants, matched well in character and versatility with Lee, Hearne and Hendren, the senior N.C.O.'s. Not perhaps in high abilities; but they did not suffer in the comparison.

Bowling apart, that leaves us with all the regulars except the wicket-keeper. It may be said, erroneously enough, that provided he is of adequate standard one wicket-keeper is virtually as good as another; the disproof of this is in the immense encouragement to a team an outstanding wicket-keeper may be (let the name of Godfrey Evans be exhibited for a moment as shining definitive example and then quickly withdrawn to get us back into the proper context). Harry Robert Murrell, known no doubt for excellent reasons, as 'Joe', the sterling regular performer for Middlesex for years before the 1914 war and for years after, was not only a solid fixture but a most valued purveyor of advice and encourage-ment, when required. Warner seems often to have used this wise old soldier as a kind of consultant, and his phlegmatic horse-sense sustained even the Commander-in-Chief at crucial moments in the campaign. Rather tall for the common model, Murrell looked like one's conventional idea of a more than usually sad-browed Roman Consul of the great days of the Republic – high beaked aquiline nose, appraising eyes, reliability radiating from him. A superb thermostat for when tensions mounted – as, during this little epic, they often did.

The vital question of the bowling remains. We have had a look at Hearne and Haig, and Lee was for years used as a handy away-swinger who could keep a length; but in 1919 these three had performed without distinction, Hearne being troubled by a finger injury, Lee being very expensive indeed, and Haig only penetrating on widely-spaced occasions. The highly erratic Gunasekara collected a few wickets, but nobody's record is anything to write home about, and there can be no serious surprise at Middlesex landing with a bump in the nether parts of the Championship table with only two suffering counties below them. The question then naturally arises – what miracle occurred in 1920 to revive their fortunes so dramatically?

Well, in the first place Hearne recovered and collected nearly four times as many wickets as he had in the bad last year. In the second place Lee was used more often and more valuably. Haig on the other hand neither came on nor fell away, just bowled with his easy graceful action to less than adequate purpose. But over and above these there were two factors, two arrivals of very great importance indeed.

The first was a genuine fast bowler. In 1919, and indeed for some years before, the county had contrived to do without this little luxury; and it will already have been made sufficiently clear that in 1919 they hadn't contrived very well. Nevertheless that year did see the arrival for a few matches of a very tall and powerful young man named Jack Durston, who struck no sparks out of Lord's or anywhere else but in whom the intervening year of training and development seemed to have effected a magical transformation.

He stood something like six feet five inches in his socks, was broad and amiable and had great strength of hip and shoulder. In the passage of time he bowled himself into a state of popular permanence at Lord's until he was almost as household a name as

Hendren or Hearne or Lee or Murrell. Banged down from the height of six feet five, with the joyous weight of youth and seventeen stone behind it, the ball began to acquire a fierce and awkward lift when Durston bowled it. This kind of bruise-and-brawn stuff when bowled by callow inexperienced youth was catsmeat to batsmen of the Hobbs-Gunn variety; but in the early weeks of the 1920 season it soon became clear that this gigantic newcomer was bowling a length and bowling on the wicket. The sighs of relief from Plum Warner are still faintly echoing to this day. Strength and attack was something in which Middlesex bowling had lately faltered and failed. Jack Durston brought back both; his success in this year and the next won him an England cap in 1921 – only one, and he really deserved more. Not that he seemed to mind; he continued loyally and cheerfully to bang them down from the upper air until age and growing girth took him into coaching. Perhaps on the average he was never among the very fastest bowlers; a lively quick medium, but the height and the weight envenomed the menace. In 1920 he was a very great asset indeed.

The other important addition to the fold was of a somewhat different order. The combined menaces of war and sickness were powerless to distract Plum Warner from vigilance among youthful and promising cricketers within the county boundaries, and his interest had been seized as early as 1918 by an altogether unusual development of talent as near home as Hampstead, though not in the familiar recognizable context of a Lord's School. It was in 1919 that a tall lad at University College School named G. T. S. Stevens achieved a place in the record-books by making as many as 466 in a house match. (One mildly wonders why he, and similar prodigies before him, A. E. J. Collins of Clifton, for example, were allowed to go on so long. At my own modest academy, which met and meets University College School on equal and pleasurable terms, a feat of this kind would have been regarded as topheavying the match and I feel that a declaration would have occurred at an earlier stage; but let that pass.) Not only did Stevens bat, but he bowled precociously, leg-breaks and googlies, and it was, during the press of war's alarms, a whole season before this record-breaking achievement, that Warner had marked down the schoolboy prodigy for his own and virtually advanced upon the school in person and carried him away under his arm.

He played him with some success in a representative war-time match at Lord's in the best company; and in the next season Stevens added his name to history by being the first schoolboy for nearly a century to play in the Gents v. Players match at Lord's. This was led up to by the prelude of his first county game, played on Whit-Monday at headquarters against Hampshire, in which he very nearly ran through the opponents on his own and took 7 for 104. If Harry Lee had not put a dolly on the grass, the bowler mildly recalled fifty years later, he would have had 8 for 80. Even so, he took ten wickets in this his first match for Middlesex; and in the Gents v. Players fixture he took a blinder to catch Mead at short-leg, picked up Alec Kennedy's wicket and made a few runs when needed. By the end of the season he had collected 21 wickets for Middlesex, and reached 50 twice. By 1920 his development had matured him into every bit as appreciable an asset as Durston. For the first part of the season he was fledging himself at Oxford; but we may be certain that Warner was delighted to have him in reserve.

These characters and talents made up the ready potentiality of the Middlesex team when the season of 1920 opened. Even before any ball had been bowled there must have been hopes at least, spoken and unspoken, for some improvement, however slight, over their ignominious thirteenth position of the year before. (This was thirteenth out of fifteen only – Worcester was not back in the list in that particular year, and Glamorgan had not yet begun their illustrious first-class history.)

The hopes may have been strengthened by a communal feeling of goodwill towards Warner, whom the 1919 failures, county and personal, had not unnaturally depressed and who had taken close counsel with his old captain A. J. Webbe, who was now the Club's President, as to whether it would be best for all if he resigned. Webbe refused to hear of it, reminding him that even though he had failed in two-day games he had always come off in the more leisurely three-day fixture, and urged him to try again for one more year, when of course the two-day nonsense was whistled down the wind and the ancient and honourable order re-introduced. It is possible that Plum didn't need much urging, and everybody was happy when he announced his intention of carrying on for one more season. Doubtless all his friends, county colleagues and well-wishers in their uncountable millions, took the opportunity to wish him good luck and to say they hoped he would win the Championship, and doubtless he replied with a happy smile and a promise to do just that, and no vestige of expectations in his mind or in theirs that there was the remotest likelihood that this cheerful good-humoured compliment could ever possibly come true. The knowledgeable and popular sports writer A. C. M. Croome did commit himself in April in the *Daily Mail* to the statement that Middlesex was 'the dark horse' of the Championship. Words, words, words, and amiably treated as such. Middlesex got on with the game; and for the summer months of their great year of 1920 upon which we now watch them embark, we can think of them constituted much as I have described – the slight spare figure of Warner leading the half dozen amateurs down the Pavilion steps, Harlequin, Free Forester, I Zingari caps abounding, the little animated knot of professionals fanning out obediently from the gate of the rabbit-hutch, gigantic Durston and gaunt sardonic Murrell standing way out above the cheerful square waddle of Lee, the cool reserved placidity of Hearne, the busy twinkling energetic Hendren.

'We few, we happy few, we band of brothers', no doubt
Warner quoted often to himself that season as the bright last
days of his life's career ran through his fingers like sand – for
Warner had an engaging emotional streak which comes up
through his own narrative, and he cherished the less subtle
heroics of our familiar poets, and this not only endears him to
me and to his posterity, but reconciles us also to such elements
of regret that there are amid the triumph – regret for time's
ruins, mainly, and the inevitable loss of good days and good
things – for we can feel assured that he, too, as we more
objectively now, lived and savoured these magnificent days
with the full consciousness of the lights and the darks in them,
and of all that that implied. And this is, in a measure, to have
lived.

The Games, 1

THUS equipped, Middlesex began the season, no doubt philosophically optimistic, picking their way. In those days counties need not play an equal number of matches with their fellows, the order of the table being decided entirely on a percentage basis (this led to certain quite outrageous anomalies, and there were certain complicated situations, into which I will not enter in detail because it will make my head spin, in which it was better to be bowled than to hit a four; this particular possibility has been removed). Middlesex were among the least ambitious, attempting only 20 matches, two more than either Worcestershire or Derbyshire; but they had only two-thirds of the physical slog undertaken by Sussex, who did well to play thirty and win as many as 18. (Derbyshire, sad to relate, lost 17 of their 18, and the other, just to put the tin hat on the story, was abandoned without a ball being bowled, and this was a match set apart for some unhappy man's benefit.) Middlesex were clearly set on a canny course, and they began their season modestly and unpretentiously, at Oxford. Nowadays a county would regard such a fixture as a cake-walk and fillet their side accordingly. Warner, no doubt, took immense nostalgic pleasure in being among the dreaming spires once more with memories buzzing in his head like bees; but the side he took down, though admittedly short of Haig and bolstered with more than one light-weight amateur, was tolerably representative. It happened that Oxford that year were rather heavily endowed, and although honours in the first innings were marginally with Middlesex (almost entirely through Hearne's bowling and Hendren and Lee's batting) the bowling got collared in the second innings by such illustrious undergraduates as D. R. Jardine, L. P. Hedges and the ubiquitous Stevens, their batting fell apart in the last stages under the menace of a powerfully-talented Australian leg-spinner named Bettington, and defeat was by as many as 139 runs. Warner did not seem to mind; no doubt the numinous air of his old University had given him comfort and serenity, and he must have taken great pleasure in Stevens' batting and Bettington's bowling, for both of these in the future were to do much in their several ways for Middlesex. (And as an interesting and almost entirely irrelevant footnote, may I remark in passing upon the enriching experience of the Oxford wicket-keeper F. W. Gilligan, who was actually dismissed in the second innings by Hendren; which he followed up a few weeks later, when Oxford visited the Oval, by being clean bowled by Hobbs.)

Perhaps in the next match the atmosphere was just that bit less relaxed; at any rate Middlesex put the screws on Warwickshire at once. It was their first appearance of the season at Lord's, the opposition was not expected to be strong, and Middlesex had put paid to them by lunch-time on the third day. The Middlesex second line of amateur bowlers did most of the damage, Gunasekara whisking through Warwickshire in the first innings and a keen but lesser-known performer named L. V. Prentice doing notable execution in the second; the batting was an expansive net practice, Hendren and Lee gobbling hundreds and Hearne 96, while Warner, doubtless

to his very great satisfaction, made 76 in helping Lee to a
first-wicket partnership of 165. He then got a fearful twinge of
cramp and had to retire; but by this time he was used to minor
inconveniences like these.

Warwick went sheepishly back to Birmingham and
Middlesex prepared for the Bank Holiday match against
Sussex, always a favourite and in those remote days a crowd-
puller. Sussex were not then quite what they had been before
the War, or what they would be a few years later when Arthur
Gilligan and Maurice Tate had developed their still latent
destructive forces, but they were a strong and attractive side.
Middlesex crushed them. Crushed them rather remarkably,
too; had them out by four o'clock on Saturday, partly through
the assiduous Prentice but chiefly through the seemingly-
innocuous Lee, who took 5 for 21 in 11 overs before waddling
off to put his pads on. He and Warner had reached 165 before
disaster struck in the Warwickshire game; in this one they got
to 241, when Lee departed with his second consecutive century
under his belt. Warner with 139 got out 43 runs later, nicking
Arthur Gilligan to the wicket-keeper; and then Haig came in
casually to his first innings of the season and made 131 in an
hour and fifty minutes, hitting twenty fours and outpacing
the staid and deliberate Hearne, who got to 116 without anybody noticing and was unbeaten when Hendren, who had been
sent in for a quick wallop, was out for 17 with the score at 543.
It is a rare thing for the first four batsmen on a side to collect
a century apiece, and up to this date it had never happened
before in first-class cricket. (It will hardly be believed, except
by cricket statisticians, that only three years later Middlesex
went and did precisely the same thing again, this time against
Hants at Southampton. Lee, H. L. Dales, Hearne and Hendren
were the joyful quartet on the second occasion; and Lee and
Hearne, who were common to both, must have felt a certain
smug satisfaction at the double feat.) In Sussex's second
innings, Lee, who seemed to have bought the match up and

made it his own, in spite of his colleagues' brilliant contributions, went clean through the late batting and put six more
wickets in his bag. And as this second innings also showed a
remarkable improvement in the bowling of Durston, whose
random energies were at last yielding to wise advice scientific-
ally proffered, Warner must have come away from the Sussex
match with something approaching the first indications of a
beatific smile.

Even so, the next game was sterner stuff altogether; the dark
inhospitable North, in the shape of a menacing Lancashire,
held them to a rather bleak draw. The Old Trafford wicket
was sluggish and unfamiliar, the fast responsive pace of Lord's
was quite lacking, the easy confidence of the prolific batsmen
broke. Only the narrowed eyes of Hearne and Hendren,
calling all skills into play, saved them from complete collapse,
and Frank Mann, whose form this summer was elusive,
played the first of two unfamiliar and invaluable innings.
Lancashire rode the difficulties more easily and Middlesex
were headed by 41; efforts to make good this lost ground were
disappointingly frustrated, and only Mann rode out the
perilous storm with an unbeaten 57 which took that mighty
hitter no less than three and a quarter hours to make. James
Tyldesley, Dick's tall fast bowler brother, took 7 for 40 and
made any kind of scoring, let alone enterprise, extremely
difficult; and when Lancashire chased 107 in the last innings,
Durston and Gunasekara found a length and fired five of their
leading batsmen out for 50. Sharp and Dick Tyldesley held
firm, nobody won or lost, the honours were even, but it was
a nasty scare to a Middlesex which was beginning to walk
proudly.

And their next match, at Nottingham, chased any faint
suspicion of pride clean out of their heads. Notts at that time
were a team of rock-solid batsmen embellished by a notable
puncher, A. W. Carr. and an unpredictable genius, George
Gunn. In Fred Barratt they had a new-ball swinger of great

potentiality – he won an England cap before he finished – and they had a burly googly-bowler named Len Richmond who had been hewn out of the living rock with a set of very generous outsize machine-tools. The weather drowned the first day and the second displayed a wicket inimical to free scoring. Durston got rid of George Gunn early on, but it was Hearne who was asked to remove the middle batting, which he dutifully and efficiently did, cutting off-spinners off the treacherous pitch and finding only the placid immovable John Gunn any sort of obstacle. Against a very modest total of 213 Middlesex never got off the ground, and allowed themselves passively to be destroyed by Barratt and Richmond. The wicket got worse; Notts had a lead of 115, and although they never found run-getting in their second innings easy they did have George Gunn, who if he really set his mind to it could get a hundred with a broom-stick on burning marl or melting ice, and he was the prime agent in ensuring that Middlesex had 260 to win. It was hopeless from the start; Warner got his fourth single-figure score in succession, the innings subsided with barely a squeak. Hendren scraped into double figures, but it was the admirable Hearne who held up the avalanche alone against the lumbering destructiveness of Richmond. Hearne remained in the ruins with high honour, 58 not out in a meagre total of 108; and Richmond, rioting among the wickets on a pitch his doctor ordered him, took 7 for 45, four of them in five bare overs. Middlesex passed into June with mixed feelings, a mild despondency for the moment predominating.

They then had three days' rest, and it seems to have done them good, the amateurs no doubt at their clubs, the professionals sallying from their rabbit-hutch for systematic practice. On Saturday 5 June, Warner won the toss against Hampshire at Lord's, the sun was shining, luck went better at last. Lee and Hendren clicked back into form again, Hendren to the tune of 183 not out, a wary and scientific piece of innings-

building, a four-hour consolidation with a firework or two in
the tail. Even the monumental steadiness of Alec Kennedy and
Jack Newman, who through the long hot twenties gave the
impression of bowling more overs and taking more wickets
for fewer runs than any corresponding pair of bowlers for any
other county, could not prevent a Middlesex total of 445;
Warner after a lean patch assisted Hendren in a fine stand of
157 and felt all the better for it; and the Hampshire batting
was simply not equal to the struggle. Mead failed twice and
Durston for the first time bowled both very fast and very
steadily, being rewarded with nine wickets in the two innings.
In Hampshire's follow-on attempt Hearne was pasted a little
by the valiant and no doubt indignant Tennyson, but he
collected five wickets and Middlesex only had to bat again to
make 14.

Another breather followed, a necessary breather one would
think, as their next opponents were Yorkshire, still at Lord's.
Yorkshire were 1919 champions; looking back on the whole of
the 1920's it is a cause of some mild surprise that this transcend-
ent side were not solidly fixed at the top of the table for the
complete decade. Even at the outset of their classic period they
are stiff with honour and renown. Holmes, Sutcliffe, Roy
Kilner, Rhodes, Robinson, Waddington, Macaulay – you can
hear trumpets sound behind the great resonant roll-call. No
Oldroyd yet, or Leyland, nor for a long time Bowes – but
already there is this almost mythical list of heroes, like names
inscribed on the shield of Achilles, that makes the tutored
blood start in answer. It started in answer all right on this
occasion, since Holmes and Sutcliffe walked out on to Lord's
and in two hours and twenty minutes put up 191 for the first
wicket. Holmes, calling the tune as he so often did, made a
lilting 149, with that brisk capable brilliance the memory of
which still stirs in Yorkshiremen – and others – the injured
unanswered question why he played so seldom for England.
A vast score seemed likely but a rain-storm destroyed con-

tinuity and cut the day's play short; Yorkshire could not recapture their tempo on the Monday, and got to 303 only, rather belatedly. Middlesex, hampered by a wet pitch and the presence of Wilfred Rhodes, could not seize their advantage. Hendren ran himself out, chivalrously, in a muddle with Warner, an early steadiness was nullified, the middle batting broke and Mann was left high and dry. It looked all up with Middlesex when Yorkshire forced a follow on, but there was a saving grace on the last day when Hearne and Hendren abode rigidly in the breach when two wickets tumbled at once. The two senior professionals stayed stolidly for two hours and put on 124; and soon after Mann launched one of his own special brands of attack and walloped everybody except Rhodes into weary ineffectuality. Hendren with 64, Mann with a satisfying 70, take credit for reducing the menace and saving the day; but most points are due to Hearne, who played classically and coolly in a day of difficulty and danger, and finished with 133 not out in just over four hours. Note, in passing, that the menace was tamed but only just; Wilfred Rhodes in the second innings took one for 35 in 35 overs against two superb England batsmen and one of the most explosive hitters of his time. Middlesex carried out of this game a surprised sensation of relief and a renewed, healthy faith in their leading batsmen.

Next day they confronted Hampshire again, the return fixture at Southampton following so hard upon the recent encounter that no doubt they were greeted with an uneasy blend of familiarity and suspicion. They had won by nine wickets at Lord's; order and symmetry prevailed and they won by nine wickets again here. Hampshire's batting improved – Mead played two fine innings of 54 and 85, Tennyson banged about him, the fifty-year old A. J. L. Hill played a classic innings of 74. Nevertheless they were swamped as they had been before; the Middlesex batting presents a picture of beautiful double-figure consistency all down the card, topped by a monumental 221 not out from Lee, who blended defence and attack with great skill for six hours. Jack Newman took none for 142, bowling like a Trojan for 37 overs; this was the measure of Middlesex's solid superiority and growing confidence.

This was further demonstrated when they took train back to Lord's and played yet another brisk return match, this time with Lancashire, who had given them such a sticky passage in Manchester barely three weeks before. The first day, predictably, was a hard grind. Warner won the toss but Lancashire gave nothing away; this time their very steady and unrelaxing bowling strength was concentrated largely – largely is the word – in the enormous expansive figure of Lol Cook, a character of portly dignity and massiveness whom Cardus once described as sweating gallons and thriving on labour and suffering. *Wisden* describes his bowling on this grilling Saturday as being like Alfred Shaw at his best, and to those to whom that magic name is only a name with no particular magic about it I should perhaps remark that in the whole history of cricket to date there can have been few more accurate bowlers than that very great Notts bowler of the 'sixties, 'seventies, 'eighties and 'nineties, who in the whole of his career bowled more overs than he had runs scored off him. Lol Cook was not consistently of this class, but he clearly had the stamp of it; and in his classic duel with the prime of the Middlesex batting this year, he tied these masters down hand and foot with his nagging perfect length. By 5.30 they had only 250 on the board; Hearne and Hendren had batted for hours, and after Cook had finally got through Hearne's defence Hendren had hung on like a dog to a bone (but *hung* on, not bashed on) and the middle batting had failed to consolidate. Haig came in at number eight, and in the last hour he and Hendren were able to cut loose when Cook's day-long accuracy began to flag. Rain moved in over the weekend, but Middlesex got to 407, Haig's admirable 84 having boosted Hendren to one of his finest innings; it is not many batsmen who, having made 183 not out on one Saturday, repeat themselves so unoriginally as to make 183 not out on another Saturday a fortnight later, but this is how Hendren slily drew attention to himself on this occasion. Cook shared the honours with him; four for 135 in 46 overs, a most memorable day's work. *Wisden* makes a point about the wicket having made a remarkable recovery after Sunday's heavy rain, but the Lancashire batting performance could hardly be excused without reference to the weather; Middlesex had them all out soon after tea on Monday for 182, Durston excelling on the freshened-up wicket and crashing through the latter end of the order like a runaway lorry. Six for 51 were his figures, a performance which must have given Warner, standing at deep point, high satisfaction as again and again the stumps were hit. In the second innings Durston refrained from monopolizing the situation and it was primarily the canny Hearne who exploited the defenders' timidity. Lancashire did barely better than in their first attempt; Durston removed Harry Makepeace twice, for 1 and 0; and the only saving Lancastrian graces were the sterling defence in each innings of Charlie Hallows and J. R. Barnes, Hallows in particular with 82 and 77 establishing a quality of easy and fluent batsmanship that was to bring him immense success over the next ten years and was to fail at the highest honours only because of a latent unadventurousness.

This match was oddly typical of much of Middlesex's summer; victory on paper looks easy and inevitable, but in the achieving it was a far tighter tussle than it seems in the bare record, and it exacted from both sides the last ounce of courage and competence to the great enrichment of the game. Thus Hendren, Haig, Durston, Hearne we might think were the decisive figures in the match; nevertheless Cook and Hallows and Barnes share the credit equally with them, and what looks like a crushing victory, or defeat, was in fact a tough trial of skills finely fought out.

Oddly enough this paradoxical ambiguity extended to the next match, whose result to all intents and purposes was the walk-over everyone expected it would be. After the Lancashire hand-to-hand a country trip to Taunton looked a happy holiday; and a ten-wicket victory on the second day looks like a happy holiday if anything does. Nevertheless it was quite otherwise at first; Somerset, a cheerful random collection of gay unpredictable amateurs bolstered with two veteran professionals past their prime, overcame early disasters and reached 184 chiefly through a lordly 75 by the classic upstanding P. R. Johnson and an impressive 38 not out from a Cambridge senior not yet thought good enough for a Blue, M. D. Lyon. The wicket did not favour the shock bowlers: Hearne it was who did much of the early damage and Lee picked up six wickets here and there. Against this mediocre total Middlesex opened disastrously, Lee this time picking up a duck, and Warner, Hearne, Mann and Kidd making 12 between them. H. K. Longman, another Old Etonian constantly on call this season, helped Hendren in a short but valuable stand, but both of them were out soon after the hundred went up, and Middlesex had seven down that night and were still over 70 behind. It never paid in the twenties to underestimate Somerset's energetic attack: Jack White had not yet reached international celebrity and excellence but was not far from it, but the damage this day was performed by the cheerful Jim Bridges, the admirable fast medium seam-bowler who for so many years alternated (at the direction of a spun coin) with Robertson-Glasgow for the honour of batting 10 or 11. Bridges had all Middlesex on the defensive on the first day – on the second he was foiled at almost the last ditch by Haig and Gunasekara, who survived, consolidated and finally broke free to add 121 for the eighth wicket. Haig's bowling went unheeded in this game, and Gunasekara had one victim only; but their respective scores of 90 and 48 decisively swayed the balance. They ensured a lead of 51; and Hearne's crafty fingers spun Somerset out again, Lyon alone shaping vigorously and effectively against him. Middlesex were asked to get 127; somewhat surprisingly, in view of the scoring difficulties characterizing this match so far, Lee and Longman got them without loss. Again, however, no walk-over; in retrospect an excellent thing, as walk-overs do not temper championship winners half so well as victories hardly fought.

The Somerset match was over on 24 June, a day early; and it is odd in the light of more recent routines to be faced with the fact that Middlesex now proceeded to enjoy a rest until 17 July. It will be remembered that they had opted to play only a very small number of Championship matches; by now they were virtually half-way through their programme, nine played, eleven to come. Lord's in the next few weeks was to be occupied with Universities playing the MCC, with the Varsity match itself, with Gents v. Players, with Eton and Harrow, with all manner of parti-coloured variations on the humdrum. Middlesex were let out to play. They came home from Taunton on 24 June and dispersed as a team just when it would seem their co-ordination had been steadily and pains-takingly achieved. Their professional batsmen were now in top gear, the fast bowler they had prayed for had been delivered spick and span, batting auxiliaries like Mann, Haig and Gunasekara had proved themselves first-class emergency men, Jack Hearne was one of the finest spinners in the country, and the fielding it appears was at this stage one of the sights of the season. Hendren, in addition to being one of the fastest runners, was the safest catcher in first-class cricket, and Gunasekara had a mercurial Oriental brilliance which labelled him among the outstanding fielders of the day. Hearne, Lee and Mann moved more slowly but never let anything past them, and Murrell's vigilance was reinforced with supreme efficiency. The whole machine was working with smooth and exhilarating precision; I find it difficult to feel that this enforced three-week rest can have been welcome. It is possible that it did Warner good; he needed to watch his stamina and his resources, his batting had recently hinted that he was tiring, and it is likely that he welcomed it (although there is no evidence available to me at this late stage to contradict the possibility that he may have spent the entire interval playing country-house cricket; I think it likelier that he occupied it with watching at Lord's). Hendren, Hearne, Durston, Lee, Haig, several others too perhaps, appeared in representative sides of major or minor importance. Hendren in particular got packets of runs out and about, and Hearne joined in too. The others I suppose went back to their clubs and house-parties; there was no doubt Wimbledon to be attended, and Ascot. It made a break, before the sterner campaigns of the second half of the summer.

And yet it does not seem at this stage that there was any particular sense of crisis or expectancy in the minds of those concerned. We can look back on it with the knowledge and wisdom of fifty years and see that this mid-season rest was in fact a *reculement pour mieux sauter*, a breather before the epic strife. Nobody of course was to know this, or even to dream it. Whether the Championship crown was actively in Warner's own ambition at this moment is impossible to guess; he has not indicated in any account of this season that I have seen that the possibility was canvassed for weeks yet. Middlesex when they knocked off for their holidays were comfortably headed by Yorkshire, Surrey, Kent and Lancashire, and hotly breathed upon by Sussex. The future was in the future, and could well be left to take care of itself. At any rate they were improving remarkably on last year, and that was something that Warner in his last season could feel comfortably proud about. It was as if they were pulling themselves up to new standards of attainment to give him a happy send-off.

It is the safest of all assumptions that he himself watched the University match. The weather attacked it brutally in an otherwise sun-bathed summer, and at least two days were spent by the teams, as the most memorably articulate of them all recorded, in playing an elaborate stump-cricket in the dressing-rooms until MCC members complained. It was a sad pity because the sides were strong and diverse – seven future England players took part as well as at least one other who ought to have been but wasn't – and several bright skills remained frustratingly undeployed. Nevertheless Warner must often, during the day and a half of truncated play, have found his eye resting with satisfaction upon G. T. S. Stevens, whom he now knew to be free to assist his county once this match was out of the way. Coming in for Oxford at number seven, Stevens, who already had an average of nearly 40 with two nineties under his belt, shored up a tottering innings with an admirable 39 and followed this up by taking 3 for 18 in seven overs, an easy all-round accomplishment that must have made his benevolent patron's mouth water where he sat; and when Cambridge batted it was his pleasure to watch the brilliant and exceptional fielding at cover point of one C. H. L. Skeet, a dour Old Pauline of unpretentious batting attainments but of electrical quality in the field, further amateur material for future, and as it turned out almost immediate, use.

So back they went into harness on 17 July at Lord's, for the one straight Championship match allotted to them there before the Schools' fortnight took over. Essex were their opponents and Warner won the toss, walking out to bat with Lee for this concluding match of the first half of their programme to face two of the most testing opening bowlers in England. Johnny Douglas and his abounding menacing energy are well known even to-day with the enduring endorsement of Jack Hobbs' avowal that Douglas was the most difficult opening bowler he ever had to face; George Louden, his partner, could on his day be quite deadly in pace and precision but never played regularly enough to establish himself as fit for the Test honours he surely deserved. To come after a long lay-off to face these two penetrating perils was an instant

confrontation with reality. Fate provided an early answer –
Douglas got Warner for a duck (one can see Warner's pained
but patient smile at his old friend and colleague) and Louden
broke past Lee's crouch at 7. The fabric quivered, but only
momentarily; Hendren and Hearne had had no holiday, they
were in full and flowering practice, and the solid professional
bats set themselves in full earnest to grind down the attack.
Douglas never gave up easily and he kept himself, and Louden,
at it hard; but there was little effective spin or flight to call in
to back them, and Hendren and Hearne did exactly what they
were paid to do. Hearne went quietly and circumspectly to
his third century of the season, methodically gauging and
measuring Douglas' powerful swing and variations of length;
Hendren, in high form this high summer, missed 100 by only
14; and when these were out Bruce and Haig added their
tally with skill and generosity and were followed by Stevens
at number eight leading what by discourtesy we must call the
tail in a fine rampage of 82 invaluable runs. Apart from the
two openers and Mann, whom Douglas got before he had
scored, the whole side made rich and invigorating contributions, and I am sure that Warner's own failure went for little
in his own mind as he watched Stevens thrashing the tired
attack. 446 was the ultimate total, and the measure of Douglas'
value to his own county can be determined by a glance at his
analysis, which was six for 114 in 29 overs. Louden bowled
even more overs, 33 in fact, had 122 runs knocked off his
bowling and dismissed nobody at all after Lee. Three other
bowlers picked up one not very economical wicket apiece,
and that is the shadowy outline of the episode of the battle of
one enormously talented and courageous bowler, virtually
single-handed, against what was rapidly becoming the best
batting side in the country.

Thanks to a brilliant destroying spell of fast bowling by
Durston, the Essex innings was almost swept away before it
was properly founded, and although the late middle batting

rallied eight wickets were down for 184 and only Jack Russell,
who had opened the innings, had any constructive idea how to
outface the speed of Durston and the spin of Hearne, upon
whom Warner was principally relying as a foil. (His newly-
arrived leg-spinner, Stevens, was sparingly used in this match.)
Russell was a tall broad aggressive player who performed so
well this year that he was put in the touring side to Australia
as Jack Hobbs' opening partner. He was less than successful
in this capacity, but he did open for England at home and in
South Africa in the few years to follow. The arrival of Sutcliffe,
it is regrettable to note, extinguished him as a Test possible;
this was hard on a fine and reliable player, although it might
be ventured that with Percy Holmes available he was mighty
fortunate ever to have had the chance. However that may be,
he was a grand county batsman and on this occasion he saved
the bacon of his own side, single-handed up to the fall of the
eighth wicket, and from then on with the unexpected help of
number ten, a loyal campaigner named L. C. Eastman, who
was to be bowler, batsman and experienced hewer of wood
and drawer of water for successive Essex sides right up until
the outbreak of the Second World War. As the Middlesex
bowling lost its sting these two took their time and nearly
doubled their side's score in a superb fighting partnership of
180. Then Russell was lbw to Hearne in a moment of weak-
ness for a score of 197 that had both courage and class; and
with Eastman out for 91 the Essex innings was over. They were
76 behind, but these two had delayed things long enough to
make it very difficult for Middlesex to contrive full points out
of the game. They went in with their back hair down and
struck sparks out of the formidable bowling in an attempt to
score enough to make a reasonable declaration possible and
victory likely. Hearne and Hendren again, with 76 and 55,
plundered Douglas and Louden, particularly Louden; Lee,
Mann and Haig all added generous portions to the common
stock. Warner for some reason did not go in, but declared with

five wickets down leaving Essex over 350 to win. As it happens he left his declaration too late; his principal bowlers, Durston and Hearne could not reproduce their earlier form – Durston had bowled over 30 overs in the first innings, and so had Hearne; moreover, the latter had scored a little matter of 200 runs in two innings – and Essex, after momentarily faltering, were stayed by Perrin and Douglas and saved the day. This draw, owing to the complex and irrational system of percentages obtaining that year, penalized Middlesex in the table, in spite of their first innings lead; and Warner, with engaging candour, confesses that when working out his declaration plans he had got his arithmetic muddled up. Indirectly this error of his may have contributed quite appreciably to the tightening tensions of the next month's story.

Once more the team had a three days' rest, and here ends the first half of this crowded campaign. The great final phase may be said to begin with the return match with Essex at Leyton on 24 July – how oddly the situation seems to have repeated itself with Middlesex this year, that a tight match with one set of opponents was almost immediately followed, before anyone could even hiccup, by a second confrontation with the same set of ditto. Let us therefore draw breath for these three days and prepare to watch the last stage even more closely, taking it match by match. Most of the games deserve it; some of them really need a whole book to themselves.

5) The Games, 2

Essex v. Middlesex at Leyton; 24, 26 and 27 July, 1920

WITHOUT any particular sense of doom or destiny upon them, Middlesex presented themselves at Leyton the Saturday following the Tuesday on which they had bidden their Essex opponents a temporary farewell. They took with them the same side as had then dispersed, with one exception. Bruce, that free, wristy aristocratic batsman, was unavailable, and for the first time in this season Skeet of Oxford came in to make up the side, batting cagily low down the order and fielding throughout the match far better than the man he replaced, or indeed most of the rest of the side, was ever able to do. Douglas won the toss, and belligerently appeared with Russell to open the innings, a kind of gauntlet-throwing gesture which one feels would have been savoured by both captains.

It was fifty years ago, and it is difficult to recapture the weather conditions from such accounts as are available; but the inevitable conclusion that one is forced to draw from a study of the score-sheet is that the recent rains had freshened up the plumb Leyton wicket and made it, especially in the early morning, susceptible to lift and spin. There is a potent tendency on the part of the batting to give at the knees without warning; a number of very good batsmen indeed did themselves no justice at all. In comparison with the Lord's game a week back the scores were laughably meagre; a number of bowlers did conspicuously well. All honour to them, and a puzzled frown towards the defaulting batsmen; I cannot avoid a mild and inquisitive glance at the pitch. Something must have been odd about it; Murrell let 39 byes.

Whoever or whatever was to blame, the Middlesex fast bowlers were all over the Essex batting before the shine was off the ball. Douglas, Russell, Freeman, Perrin and Morris were swept into the bin before the score had reached thirty – Douglas snapped at the wicket, Russell in the slips, Freeman clean bowled, Perrin lbw, Durston doing the prime damage and bowling very steadily, conceding nothing. The veteran amateurs McIver and McGahey set themselves to combat this aggression; Warner switched his attack, replacing the openers with Hearne and Lee; the two Macs got their experienced heads down and batted with astuteness and care, adding an invaluable 70 before Hearne clean bowled them both, one after the other. The rest of the batting made very little headway against Lee, who picked up three cheap wickets among the tail-enders. 133 was the total; derisory in some contexts, but wise heads figured that this was not one of them. They had taken time and pains over it; runs in this match were not to be had for the easy asking.

Warner retaliated in a measure to Douglas' opening batsman gesture by sending in Haig to partner Lee. George Louden fired him out at once; this was no time for gestures. Lee and Hearne buckled down bleakly to what looked like being a tough struggle against the collar; we are now in the second day, Monday 26 July, and here an unusual extraneous pressure makes itself felt.

This winter, 1920–21, was the winter of the first Australian tour by an MCC side since the War; excitement was beginning to simmer up, the captain, Johnny Douglas, had already been chosen, and Monday 26 July was the date fixed for the meeting of the Selection Committee to deliberate the choice of players. There were, incidentally, many who felt that English cricket had not yet rehabilitated itself sufficiently after the War to make such an early tour of Australia desirable. Natural keenness and natural goodwill swept aside objections that had many points in their favour; it is for cricket-lovers to judge for themselves, if they can, and if it matters now, whether the five crushing Test defeats, which our players endured when they got there, and which have so far never been rivalled in consistency by any other touring side, constitute an adequate hindsighted argument against the tour, or whether defeat or victory really count much alongside the praiseworthy reestablishment of the admirable series itself. In July 1920 optimism was very properly in the air; and although Warner himself was not a member of the Selection Committee, he had been asked by Lord Harris its Chairman to come to Lord's on the afternoon of 26 July to help in the choosing.

The relevance of this arrangement pressed home upon him when with Haig and Hearne out and the situation dodgy, the luncheon interval arrived on the Monday while he and Lee were busy shoring up fragments against the potential ruins. Warner himself had his nose well down and was taking comfortable root; his score stood at 22, and Lee at the other end was showing signs of settling into a familiar permanence. Still, there was nothing for it; his promise had to be kept; with natural reluctance he forfeited his innings. Some slight compensation may be noted here in that Douglas himself, likewise due at the meeting, was removed from the firing line, which induces the reflection that the Chairman of the Selection Committee might well have chosen some more convenient time for his crucial session. However, Warner was constrained to depart to Lord's, mercifully ignorant of the melancholy fact that immediately his back was turned Hendren and Mann were summarily outed and the puny Essex score not yet equalled.

The upstanding Stevens came in at this stage and relieved the tension; Mann as vice-captain, naturally anxious to present Warner on his return with a reasonable lead, must have breathed more easily at the sight of his tall youthful confidence balancing Lee's canny experience. Warner had used Stevens' bowling very sparingly in this match, possibly recalling that in the previous game at Lord's the Essex batsmen had made a light meal of him; but it was comforting to know that if he failed on one cylinder he could fire very satisfactorily on the other, and his innings of 36 helped to turn the tide. He was not yet, of course, the commanding player that, at his best, he was for some years in the twenties, with a vigilant short-back-lifted defence and powerful cuts and drives; but for a nineteen-year-old he was skilful and reliable enough and the two Essex games are but a foretaste of the strength he was to provide in the rib-cracking month to follow.

Stevens got out, Skeet and Gunasekara got out, Murrell offered a sample of his admirable quality, Durston came in just above the roller. All the time Lee was unobtrusively storing away runs, busy, unmemorable, thrifty, more than his weight in precious metal. He was left stranded when Durston got out, carrying his bat right through the innings, 80 to his name, one of his worthiest exploits in a great season. Warner has said, and he should know, and probably at this precise instant of time was airing the topic at Lord's, that Lee only very narrowly missed selection for Australia that summer. One can have one's own opinion about the actual range and extent of this excellent cricketer's capacity, and nobody need trouble now to argue whether he would have been a right choice or not. Yorkshiremen, with Percy Holmes in mind, would have voiced dissonant opinions had he been chosen; as it was he missed it – let us regard the nearness of the miss as a tribute to his superb consistency and invaluable services to his county that summer.

Middlesex led in the upshot by 79 runs, a very comfortable margin on a wicket that was never easy and early showed signs of breakage. The second Essex innings was better than the first, resolving itself virtually into a battle of wit and skill between the accredited batsmen on one side and Hearne, all by himself, on the other. It is at this part of the season that this frail and fastidious-looking man revealed himself as consistently tireless and resourceful. He had made his bowling reputation before the War with his leg-break and googly; after his finger-injury of 1919 he seems, as *Wisden* suggests, to have lost confidence in leg-spin, and although he did not give it up he relied on good length off-breaks varied by an occasional cutter. With this highly effective armoury he confronted Essex and contained them; Lee and Durston were steady, but Douglas, Russell and particularly Perrin were able to score with reasonable freedom, Lee taking most of the punishment. The rest of the innings was dealt with by Hearne, who collected most of his wickets by stumpings or catches at slip, clearly confusing the batsmen with both flight and spin. Durston bowled a most honourable stint of 24 overs for 37 runs and one wicket; Hearne bowled 27 overs and had 8 for 49. The total was 196, which left Middlesex a bare 118 to win.

Nobody with Warner's experience or temperament would have been over-confident about this, nor was he, and he still had obscure qualms of regret for the necessity that had compelled him to cut his innings short the day before. He knew, nobody better, that he was up against two very considerable bowlers on a wicket that wasn't going to improve; Hearne had been turning it with ominous ease. His basic faith in his fine batting side may never have faltered; but in a basic faith there is surely room for peripheral doubts, and any he had were stirred early when Douglas began to bowl at his best. Dark, pugnacious, shiny-haired, the Essex captain was a vivid and dynamic figure, animating his whole eleven with his own uncompromising aggressiveness. He had a long high-stepping run and superb body-action, and Jack Hobbs is not the only one to have avowed a dislike of his superb swing and nip at the start of an innings. Moreover in this last innings of the game he had something to bowl for, and in particular he had reserves of energy boxed up in him through having had to waste good bowling-time in committee at Lord's on the previous day. Little wonder then that the Middlesex batsmen sensed a virulent menace at once. 118 began to seem a very long way off indeed.

It was as bad as they thought it might be. Lee, Hearne, Hendren, Haig, Mann, Stevens – he shot them all out as soon as they were in. Lee and Haig were clean bowled, and so was Stevens; the characteristic pace of the wicket, aided by Douglas' special whip from the off, beat them on the back stroke. The rest were plumb lbw, rapped hard on the pad before the bat could get down. Hendren made 5 and 3, Haig 3 and 6, Mann 0 and 2, Hearne 16 and 6; four present, past and future England batsmen with 41 runs between them in eight innings; blame the wicket, the crisis, what you will, but allot the credit to the superb bowling. Douglas did the effective damage, but the very fast and accurate Louden pinned them to the back of their creases – he bowled 43 overs in this match for 60 runs only, there's top-class bowling for you. When the sixth wicket fell the score was only 33, and Warner, 1 not out only, popped up a ball straight into the hands of forward short leg, who put it on the grass. The imagination focuses after fifty years not so much on the lonely but relieved figure in the Harlequin cap as on the fulminating gesticulations of the enraged Douglas, who was not one to restrain either his gestures or his language on occasions like these. Warner remained, summoning all his knowledge and tradition to his task, farming the bowling, contriving if he could to take as much of Douglas as he could to shield his junior partners from this hungry enthusiastic destroyer. Skeet stayed with him a little, Warner scoring by taps and tickles, Skeet barely scoring at all; the total crept up past 50. Russell suddenly trapped Skeet lbw; Gunasekara came in, normally a random free-hitting batsman but to-day content under instructions to leave his captain to do the scoring. Warner assumed control as for weeks he had not seemed able – if any innings he played this season could be called a captain's innings, this one could. The duel between him and Douglas was in the classic pattern – energetic intelligent bowler, wary intelligent batsman, every-thing at stake, neither giving an inch; Warner poured all his sapping strength into the effort. At 67 Louden clean bowled Gunasekara; 118 seemed still a very long way off. The wily impassive Joe Murrell, friendly and unshakeable, was a very comforting partner to have join him at this moment.

Murrell not only stayed in, but he did more than his share of run-getting. He had contributed handsomely in the first innings; in the second he improved on this. Whether he had any sneaking recollection in his mind of the odd little un-characteristic matter of 39 byes cannot now be verified; he saw to it, however, consciously or otherwise, that he emerged from the match with a credit balance. He was nobody's fool as a batsman; he was tall with a long reach and a judicious eye. This hot afternoon he used both. The tension mounted higher and higher as he settled himself and the heady Essex jubilation cooled and steadied.

Warner and Murrell added 35; Warner, bent on taking Douglas, was confined mainly to defence. Murrell at the other end watched for the loose one from Eastman or Russell and hit it hard. He was a powerful man, and a four from him travelled nearly as quickly as a four from Hendren; between defence and careful opportunist attack the score heaved itself through the nineties into three figures, which looked con-siderably better. The sun blazed down over East London, the bowlers shone and sweated, the batsmen's hands were sticky in their gloves. Warner's spirit was high but he began to feel very tired. He still kept to the end facing Douglas, whom nothing exhausted.

At 102 Russell beat Murrell's careful defensive shot, and the fifth lbw decision of the innings went down in the book. Murrell's 23 was a monument more lasting than bronze; as he took his eager shrewd vigilant way back to the Pavilion Warner knew he was on his own now, for Durston was as yet no bat. There was no lack of courage and good sense, merely of skill, which he kept for bowling; to-day he used all the courage and good sense he had, playing solidly down the line with his customary expression of unalterable amiability.

By this time the stuffing was running out of Warner's boots. It is he himself in his memoirs who swears he could have lasted if he could only have had a drink 'with something in it'. It had been years before when feeling, as he so often did, a good deal below par one day, he absorbed for the first time in his life a strong brandy-and-soda at twelve o'clock noon and followed it up with an even stronger one at lunch; the stimulus carried him that day to 244, the highest score of his life. This time he could have done with a modest nip; he was virtually all in; but the licensing laws of the day did not permit the bar to oblige him until opening hours. He does not repine, but he wonders; and in the upshot the younger man prevailed. With the score at 113, with only five needed to win, the indefatigable Douglas went through him with a yorker. Essex had won, but cricketing honours were even; a splendid match had called out the last reserves of determination and stamina. Douglas and Warner walked in together, the one smiling happily, the other sadly; it was Douglas' superb 7 for 47 in 24 overs that had won Essex the victory, just as Warner's 46 of character and patience and resource had only just failed to win it for Middlesex.

Middlesex went home the losers, but there was less sense of disappointment and frustration than there might have been later. Warner himself says few of them at that moment had any Championship notions in their heads, although Stevens has lately reported that it was at Leyton that a knowledgeable Pressman hinted to them that if they won eight more matches they would come out top. Warner cherished the vague hope that they might get into the first three – but who, particularly encumbered as they all were by a percentage system that seemed to be at the mercy of wind and weather, could possibly have ventured in late July on any sort of prediction? 'Perhaps', says Warner philosophically, reviewing the amazing end of this unusual season, 'it is just as well that we did not realize it.' To which one answers with an emphatic Hear, Hear; this game is not devised for cardboard calculations; upon its ultimate imponderability rests half its gossamer charm. Middlesex, in the best spirits possible, went away from Leyton sorry that they could not have won the game, but (I am sure) the better for the clean bright skills with which the great cricketers involved in it had played it out. It was the first of a notable series of altogether unusual contests.

Score:

ESSEX

J. W. H. T. Douglas c Murrell b Durston	2	c Hearne b Lee	36
A. C. Russell c Lee b Durston	2	b Hearne	26
J. Freeman b Haig	3	c Hendren b Durston	8
P. Perrin lbw b Durston	8	c Hendren b Hearne	50
C. D. McIver b Hearne	43	b Hearne	23
H. M. Morris b Hearne	3	st Murrell b Hearne	17
C. McGahey b Hearne	44	c Gunasekara b Hearne	1
J. G. Dixon lbw b Lee	1	c Warner b Hearne	0
L. C. Eastman c and b Lee	0	st Murrell b Hearne	2
G. M. Louden b Lee	2	lbw b Hearne	1
F. Scoulding not out	0	not out	0
B 15 lb 10	25	B 24 lb 7 nb 1	32
	133		196

	O	M	R	W		O	M	R	W
Haig	15	8	15	1		4	0	20	0
Durston	16	9	16	3		24	11	37	1
Lee	12.2	3	25	3		22	4	58	1
Hearne	12	2	33	3		26.4	5	49	8
Gunasekara	4	2	2	0					
Stevens	5	0	17	0					

MIDDLESEX

N. Haig b Louden	3	b Douglas	6
H. W. Lee not out	80	b Douglas	9
J. W. Hearne b Eastman	16	lbw b Douglas	6
P. F. Warner retired	22	b Douglas	46
E. Hendren c Louden b Eastman	5	lbw b Douglas	3
F. T. Mann b Louden	0	lbw b Douglas	2
G. T. S. Stevens c McCahey b Scoulding	36	b Douglas	3
C. H. L. Skeet run out	2	lbw b Russell	5
Dr. C. H. Gunasekara b Scoulding	6	b Louden	4
H. R. Murrell b Scoulding	18	lbw b Russell	23
F. J. Durston c Freeman b Eastman	3	not out	1
B 8 lb 13	21	B 4 nb 1	5
	212		113

	O	M	R	W		O	M	R	W
Douglas	4	2	2	0		24.2	5	47	7
Louden	18	6	28	2		25	10	32	1
Scoulding	19	1	59	3		3	0	8	0
Eastman	17.3	1	58	3		2	1	5	0
Russell	14	1	44	0		10	5	16	2

Essex won by 4 runs

Sussex v. Middlesex at Hove, 31 July and 2 August, 1920

Middlesex's fixture list is prodigal of three-day rests about this time; and they had one following the Essex match. Warner, one could imagine, needed every minute of it after his con-

centrated exertions; and all would hope that he made the
most of it, since from 31 July onwards there was to be no more
lay-off until the end of the season a month hence. I am prepared to bet that he spent two of the days watching his old
school play Marlborough at Lord's; the weather was un-
inviting, the hot spell having broken up into sweeping rain,
and most cricket arranged during this week suffered serious
interference. (I know this personally; Friday 30 July happened
to be my eighth birthday, and a picnic and cricket match that
had been arranged were drowned out; fifty years later I catch
across the abysses of time a faint savour of my disappointment.)

On 31 July, the Saturday before Bank Holiday, Middlesex
began their traditional holiday fixture against Sussex at Hove.
The invigorating salt airs pervade this match with a characteristic tang; the trippery atmosphere of the greatest of all
English watering-places invests the county and the cricket
with a lively and stimulating charm. Middlesex remembered
with pleasure, Sussex doubtless without, that the Whitsuntide
encounter at Lord's had almost crushed the life out of the
seaside county; and four Middlesex batsmen at the top of the
order savoured the rather attractive prospect of having another
try at a century apiece. However, when the Saturday dawned
the aftermath of the recent rainy weather had damped the tang
in the air, the sky was overcast and the wicket was puddingy
to the touch. Rainclouds hovered in the offing, and H. L.
Wilson, the zealous and workmanlike Sussex captain, decided
to bat when he beat Warner in the toss, for there was little life
in the turf and he hoped to collect some quick runs while it
was still unresponsive.

Who can trust English weather? The clouds sheered off
before the game was half an hour old. Warner never used
Haig at all; Lee was Durston's opposite number with the new
ball, and the capable Vallance Jupp and the veteran Joe Vine
weathered this conventional attack with no great difficulty. It
was Durston who got the first two wickets – Jupp gave a

catch to Warner at point, and Bowley followed almost at once, snapped up by Stevens close to the wicket; but by this time Warner had begun to play with the controls – first Hearne came on, then Stevens. The sun shone brighter, the big gay holiday crowd prepared to enjoy itself expansively for the first time for years, and to the deep delight of the Middlesex captain and team the wicket began to bubble and fester in the genial heat. Warner must have purred gently to himself at point, watching Stevens strike a length at once, justifying his own faith, his own patience in awaiting his arrival during the season, his own pride in his acumen in fostering him. Plum Warner seemed to stand *in loco parentis* to so many, indeed to all of his banded followers, that to single out one above the others is perhaps wrong-headed – and yet one seems to sense that during this latter half of this last season he cherished this superb young cricketer like a son, for he was by far the youngest of his team, yet one of the most variously endowed, rejoicing in his new vigour and capacity to match his skill with the greatest.

On that morning and early afternoon of Bank Holiday Saturday Stevens decided the result of the match. Sussex shredded into helpless fragments before him; there was not a single batsman who had any answer to him at all. The sturdy Test experience of Joe Vine held him watchfully at his post as long as it could; but the young leg-spinner used his height so commandingly to impart the extra spring and bounce from what must have been an exceptionally vicious wicket that complete disintegration could only have been a matter of time. Not very much time, either; the massacre was complete, at any rate at Stevens' end, in a matter of eight overs. Wilson bravely and desperately let down a temporary anchor, Tate and Arthur Gilligan made perfunctory gestures of defiance, but it was no good. Half-way through Saturday afternoon the whole side was sunk for 92, and Stevens had taken, in the course of those eight modest overs, 7 for 17. It was doubtless during

the heady closing passages of this lamentable innings that the
Leyton journalist's hint began to grow in Warner's stimulated
imagination into a possibility. The rest of the day could only
have confirmed him in his optimism.

Plum himself was the last man alive to allow personal failure
and disappointment to cloud his pleasure in the common
success, and I cannot think that he permitted himself a sleepless
night on this occasion, even though Arthur Gilligan's formidable pace removed him at once for a duck. The years had
taught him philosophical resignation by now; the incident
could well be regarded as closed when he could sit comfortably
back in the pavilion and watch the confident bats of Lee and
Hearne wearing down the early penetrative thrusts and
advancing against the bowling in strong counter-attack.
Gilligan, Tate, Albert Relf, Jupp are ominously loaded names –
but on closer scrutiny it would be fair to remember that in 1920
Relf was falling from his peak and his very honourable and
illustrious colleagues had hardly reached theirs. A name is a
name but its bearer is subject to Time's immaturities and
Time's encroachments; to play Tate with ease in 1920 was one
thing, but let the same player try to do the same thing four
years later. . . . This time Lee and Hearne had skills in hand in
plenty, and the wicket had perversely rolled out true; they put
on 144 in two hours, and Hearne with 54 was the only other
batsman to get out that night. Hendren on Bank Holiday
showed the Brighton crowds agreeably and mercilessly what
his idea of a Bank Holiday was, hunting up and down the
wicket for runs, seeing Lee to a century and only falling 12
short of one himself; Mann followed expansively in and hit
three consecutive sixes off Tate (in respect of which please
refer to what I have already remarked about that bowler a few
lines back) and Stevens added an agreeable twenty or so just
to re-record his presence in the party before Warner declared
277 runs ahead in the happiest of all possible moods. There was
a day and a half to play with; and although the evil in the

wicket had apparently abated while Middlesex were batting, there was sufficient margin to allow Sussex plenty of improvement and yet still to beat them in comfort. Sussex, caught from the beginning on the wrong foot, appeared to agree; they did a little better than they had contrived to do in the first innings, but not very much, and the prevailing impression left by the sight of the score-sheet is that each batsman permitted himself a couple of holiday fours before acknowledging that further resistance was useless. The fact that they made 154 in only two hours and a quarter suggests a carefree surrender rather than a grim losing battle; one can picture Maurice Tate's 21, a cheerful clump or two and an amiable grin, or Harold Gilligan's 33, a dashing and debonair flicker of adventurous grace without much solid foundation from one of the most attractive of Sussex amateurs – and most of the others collected their modest double-figure totals, to little substantial avail. This time Stevens bowled more overs, and the cheerful holiday batsmen took a few more runs off him; Durston, bowling fast at the other end, was plainly having a minor off day, and when he dropped short they hit him. Hearne bowled tightly on a severe length; but by the end of the afternoon Stevens had all the last words. The batsmen scored off Durston and were bottled up by Hearne, but it was Stevens, still extracting bounce for his leg-spin from a wicket that was now showing signs of wear and tear, who found the penetrative power necessary to complete the destruction. Six for 43 in 13 overs gave him a match record of 13 wickets for 60 in 21 overs less one ball; a memory which one would expect him to cherish in pleasurable contentment all his life, and it is of interest to note that his modest comment fifty years later was that even if he hadn't bowled a single ball Middlesex would have won all the same.

That is, I suppose, as it may be; he observed the quality of the Sussex batting and bowling, and I did not; but there is no doubt to whom the Man of the Match award would have gone, if such noxious practices had prevailed in those days. The

Bank Holiday crowd got its Bank Holiday cricket; but Tuesday was left blank, and Middlesex got a day's earned rest before facing a much more formidable set of opponents.

Score:

SUSSEX

V. W. C. Jupp c Warner b Durston	11	b Durston			12
J. Vine c Haig b Stevens	28	c Hendren b Stevens			11
E. H. Bowley c Stevens b Durston	2	c Hendren b Durston			17
R. Relf c Durston b Hearne	6	b Stevens			11
H. L. Wilson b Stevens	19	c Hearne b Stevens			2
M. W. Tate c Durston b Stevens	9	c Murrell b Stevens			21
A. E. Relf c Hendren b Stevens	0	c Murrell b Stevens			2
A. E. R. Gilligan c Murrell b Stevens	6	c Skeet b Stevens			2
A. H. H. Gilligan b Stevens	0	b Durston			33
G. Cox c Haig b Stevens	1	b Hearne			21
G. Street not out	1	not out			0
B 6 lb 3	9	B 16 lb 4 nb 2			22
	92				154

	O	M	R	W	O	M	R	W
Durston	13	3	30	2	10.2	1	54	3
Lee	7	1	17	0	7	2	14	0
Hearne	5	1	19	1	8	2	15	1
Stevens	7.5	2	17	7	13	3	43	6
Gunasekara					8	7	6	0

MIDDLESEX

P. F. Warner b A. E. R. Gilligan	0	F. T. Mann b Cox	44
H. W. Lee c Vine b A. E. Relf	132	G. T. S. Stevens lbw b Cox	22
J. W. Hearne lbw b Jupp	54	C. H. L. Skeet c Vine b Cox	0
E. Hendren c A. E. Relf b Tate	88	H. R. Murrell not out	1
N. Haig c and b A. E. Relf	1	B	22
Dr. C. H. Gunasekara c A. E. R.			
Gilligan b A. E. Relf	5	(9 wkts dec)	369

F. J. Durston did not bat

	O	M	R	W
A. E. Relf	20	7	51	3
A. E. R. Gilligan	28	10	57	1
Tate	25.4	9	90	1
Cox	36	9	82	3
Jupp	10	4	27	1
Wilson	1	0	3	0
A. H. H. Gilligan	6	0	30	0
R. Relf	2	1	7	0

Middlesex won by an innings and 123 runs

Kent v. Middlesex at Canterbury, 4, 5, and 6 August, 1920

This match was destined from the start, and nobody knew this
better than Warner, to be an altogether tougher proposition.
Sussex in this season were an uneasy combination of declining
veterans and immature young players of promise, who had
ventured ambitiously on a too comprehensive programme.
Kent, far more firmly co-ordinated, were comfortably endowed with highly reliable batsmen and slow bowlers, the
latter enjoying the benefits of uncertain weather so enthusiastically that their successes almost entirely cancelled out the
severe handicap of having no fast bowler whatever. Kent also
rejoiced in the possession of a genius, the measure of whose
capacity may be gauged by the fact that while we nowadays
delight to honour Frank Woolley for his supremely graceful
and commanding batsmanship, in this year of 1920 he actually
collected 185 wickets (164 in Championship matches alone) in
addition to his little matter of nearly 2,000 runs. With this
asset, plus a little luck, and the hugely successful googly
bowler Tich Freeman thrown in, Kent were one of those sides
who could be pardoned for expecting to be able one of these
fine days to close their eyes and have the Championship
dumped into their laps; and they had lately reinforced their
pardonable superiority-complex by murdering, in very quick

succession, such brassbound and heavily-fortified opponents as Yorkshire, Surrey and Hampshire. Surrey in particular, in a season of great confidence and success for them, had been submitted at Blackheath, then and always their unfavourite ground, to a most dismal humiliation, being put out twice in a very few hours without Freeman having to bowl more than one over. The wet weather in late July had played into Kent's cunning hands; and they came to the second match of the Canterbury Week with a substantial victory over their first opponents, Hampshire, to cheer them as well as the reinforcing knowledge that in the last four matches Woolley had taken 31 wickets and made 306 runs.

The Canterbury Week was at its shimmering height when Warner brought his team to the St. Lawrence ground. To-day much of its characteristic lustre has been dimmed; but then it stood perhaps as the nearest equivalent in genuine first-class cricket to the high Edwardian epitome of country-house opulence and grace. Tents were pitched around and beyond the immemorial oak; flags and pennants waved above the marquees, the sunlight glinted on the band's instruments and accoutrements, the cigar-smoke drifted above the canvas. Band of Brothers, Old Stagers, I Zingari, Kentish Men, the St. Lawrence Club – the tents and their companionable occupants glittered and pullulated in the noonday – a provincial Eton and Harrow match, a thing of rendezvous and reunion, of strawberries and cream and champagne, of parasols, of smart outfits and summer hats, Chelsea Flower Show without the flowers, Ascot without the horses, a faint but pervasive smell of beer coming up through the wreathings of tobacco-smoke; all summer and a day, whatever the weather; and between the eager and garrulous heads and shoulders, the white figures on the green, the great Cathedral only just round the corner and the garden of England all around. What better setting for the bright-eyed nostalgic Warner, coming slowly to his culmination like a ship to the end of its voyage?

Warner won the toss, but it is possible that he soon wished that he hadn't. The damp airs of late July had given an unpredictable bite to the wicket, and Woolley and Fairservice were by now happily used to these conditions. This time Lee took in as opening partner H. L. Dales, a circumspect left-hander with great sweeping ears, who was to make many a century stand with him in the decade to come. This time he failed and so did Lee; Hearne and Warner were not very long in following them home. Warner, improving by one run on his Hove duck, may have begun at this stage to have private, even public, doubts about the Leyton journalist's cheerful hint; and when Mann fell to Freeman very soon after and half Middlesex were out before lunch, he must have got ready to bear disappointment with the gay stoicism which he had at his command on and off the cricket field his whole life long. Hendren, however, was by this time well dug in; and Warner could be thankful at this ticklish stage for the iron resolution that was hidden beneath the airy freedoms of Haig's batting. It was characteristic of that amused and amusing personality to offer his very best when, and only when, disaster threatened if he didn't; on this day at Canterbury he would have stood by Thomas Becket and defied the murderers with wit and with success. Before Woolley picked him up at slip he had scored as valuable a fifty as anyone ever saw him score; and after a little resistance from Stevens the sand ran out of the rest of the side, Woolley collecting up the last wickets with perfunctory ease and leaving Hendren without a partner at 77 not out. 212 was no dishonourable total; but it was nothing whatever for a captain to be sanguine about.

If he did feel sanguine he gave it up very shortly; for Kent showed early signs of taking root. Warner began by switching his bowlers about, playing no doubt for variety and distraction; the active and lively Gunasekara of Ceylon began the attack with Durston, but he had him off soon, and ran up and down the scale like a musical improvisation, trying six bowlers

before he even considered using Haig. As it happened it was
Dales, who normally never bowled except as a joke, who got
the first wicket quite early, removing the elegant Bickmore
for 8; but there were not to be any more successes that night.
Two of the toughest professional batsmen in sub-Test cricket,
Wally Hardinge and James Seymour, got down on their bats
at once in the most workmanlike manner possible. Tough,
compact, prolific, Hardinge was a mainstay at the top of the
Kent order for years and years, free and quick-footed, a county
treasure, unlucky like many others who could be named to be
used so little for his country, who called on him precisely once.
Admittedly any aspiring opening batsman living in the
consulship of Hobbs and Sutcliffe could normally have sold
his England prospects for sixpence; Wally Hardinge perforce
concentrated his enormous talents into county cricket, and
Kent were appropriately comforted, even if he wasn't. James
Seymour, a quiet neat batsman of unobtrusive elegance and
great tenacity, had just had a benefit against Hampshire,
enjoying the contradictory experience of being run out for a
duck in the first innings and making over 70 in the second;
he was later to elevate this benefit into a celebrated action at
law, in which with Lord Harris' influential help he fought and
defeated the Inland Revenue's claim to tax his benefit-
moneys, a critical moment in the history of the tenuous
relation between our intricate and fascinating game and our
even more intricate and fascinating fiscal system. His name
should accordingly be honoured as much by cricketers when
they pocket their cheques as by veteran Kent supporters
recollecting Seymour's efficiency and charm. He, like Hardinge,
was of vintage Kent quality; and Warner, watching these two
admirable professional performers playing the whole of his
considerable range of bowlers plumb in the middle of their
quietly confident bats (let alone recollecting in his more
thoughtful moments that Frank Woolley was due to come in
next) has confessed that this was one of the stages in this close

P.W.—6

and unrelaxing game when he almost gave the match, and most of the hopes of the Championship, up for lost.

Kent that night were only 60 to 70 runs behind the Middlesex total, with but one wicket lost; Warner no doubt slept philosophically and waited for the morning's luck, but spirits cannot have been high. Yet this match was to be one of intricate checks and balances; nothing was to get out of hand; equilibrium, at times nerve-racking, was to be maintained throughout. Seymour went first; Stevens, whom the Canterbury conditions were not favouring like the Brighton ones, got him caught for 73, his only victim in the innings; and the Middlesex attackers all tightened their belts another notch to prepare for whatever overwhelming experience the arrival of Woolley might entail. The balances being set as they were, they were lucky that it did not on this occasion entail much.

There followed almost immediately one of the admirable inexplicabilities that endow the progress of a cricket season with so much of its arresting charm. Haig on the previous evening and on the present morning had, as soon as ever Warner had got round to him, continued to move in to bowl on his familiar easy run and free attractive action with no great prospect of success. He was never a bowler to vary pace or system, preferring to run comfortably in a steady groove and to rely on length and movement off the wicket to bring him his victim. Hearne at the other end exploited without result his subtlest variations; Haig's smooth automatism proceeded easily and smoothly for ten economical overs; Woolley and Hardinge seemed entirely unperturbed; and yet in the twinkling of an eye all was remarkably changed.

In six overs and one ball Haig finished off the innings; he got rid of Hardinge for 82 and Woolley for a mere 18, and after that there was nothing but a hurrying to and fro of batsmen. At this late time it is difficult to hit on an explanation for this unusual collapse – but the weather was moist, Haig could swing the ball, the dampness doubtless toned up the surface so that in the morning freshness he bit back or away with just that extra touch of venom, and feeble batting contributed to the general surprise. In those six overs they scraped 14 runs off him and he took seven wickets; Hearne collected the other one and Kent had a five-run lead only – a rousing rejuvenator for Warner's optimism, and further evidence of the extraordinary all-round potentiality of his happily co-ordinated team. If it wasn't one who came off at need, it was another; if it wasn't Lee it was Hearne, if it wasn't Hendren it was Stevens, if it wasn't Mann or Durston it was Warner himself or Haig. A balanced menacing team of great variety of talent had been evolved under Warner's quiet but dominating leadership; and it was odd that even at this late stage they could move so masterfully and yet always seem to carry two light-weights. They never had a settled partner for Harry Lee; and at number eight or nine there seemed to be a constant flux of moderate if enthusiastic second-raters. Of these the best perhaps were Gunasekara and Skeet, for they were both of supreme value in the field.

Warner's rising hopes took another whipping in the second innings, which was an unimpressive parody of the first. The openers failed again before Woolley. Hearne could not consolidate, and Hendren once more rode the tide alone. This time, however, there was no immediate rally; Freeman, five foot nothing, all nose and grin, spinning viciously on a wicket that was beginning to cut up, chewed the middle out of the batting by doing the hat trick with Hearne, Mann and Haig, and Stevens came in to join Hendren with the score at 47 for 6. Warner, back in the pavilion with a duck to follow up his first innings single, records this as the second moment in the game when he quietly buried his Championship aspirations; but his native resilience must have been bolstered early when he saw Stevens and Hendren batting with some success to restore the common fortunes. If either had got out at once

Kent must surely have won that night; but they stayed long enough to bring the total up to three figures, and the final total of 127 was enough, just enough, to keep hope alive.

Flickeringly alive only; for Kent's openers, setting cheerfully out upon what might seem the not very difficult task of scoring 123, met the Middlesex attack confidently enough. It was the Oxford batsman Bickmore this time who took chief charge of the run-getting, leaving Hardinge far behind in the tally as the openers moved without difficulty into the fifties. This was not Durston's match – he took no wickets at all – and Haig's second innings performance showed no signs of matching his first. Only Hearne struck a length, and as so often before in this match the dampness enhanced natural bowling skills to unusual heights. Warner very soon sensed that he should persevere with Hearne; and with the score in the late fifties this bowler repaid him by removing Hardinge.

Seymour started every bit as confidently as he had in the first innings. He was not a quick scorer but he had, to an opponent, a quite infuriatingly impeccable defence, and he was content to let Bickmore produce the strokes while he settled himself to make an easy victory easier. There was a full day in hand, there was all the batting time in the world, the batsmen were happy and well set, Woolley was still to come. Seymour and Bickmore set themselves to weather the last hour; the *coup de grace* could be delivered early next morning. Seventy went up, the runs came by ones and twos. Warner chronicles this precise moment as the third of those during this match when his hopeful spirit almost conceded defeat. I am prepared to bet a large sum that he did not let his side, or his opponents, guess his mind; but went on methodically switching his bowlers at the end opposite Hearne's, approving the while the dead accuracy of the latter's tight aggressive off-spinners, slung in on a low difficult trajectory and varied with the occasional one whipping from leg. It was to Hearne that he instinctively looked for positive action this time – how

miraculous that whatever the fluctuations there was always
one, no matter who, to come up with what was required.

At this depressed point in Warner's meditations, Stevens
bowled Seymour a full toss. Seymour quite properly gave it
the meat, but at the same time he allowed it the slightest bit
too much air; it departed on a flat humming parabola towards
the mid-wicket boundary, and the vivid Gunasekara, taking
off in a flash from deep square leg, took a glorious catch,
going flat out, at the level of his knees – yet another example of
the brilliant adaptability of this wonderfully co-ordinated side.

Woolley was not entirely fit, and was for the time held
back; but, as in the first innings, the first major breakthrough
heralded a calamitous decline. Hearne was deservedly the
beneficiary of some rather indifferent batting; Hubble and
Lionel Hedges in their several ways were quite unable to cope
with the additional hostility that the sudden success had
imparted to the Middlesex bowling. Hearne bowled Bickmore
for an admirable 51, and with only half an hour of the day's
play left Woolley had to come in after all. The score was 90,
five wickets were down, one of the best batsmen in the world
was approaching the wicket, and a finish which had promised
to be a comfortably amiable walk-over now loomed in prospect
as something promising all manner of anxiety. And at this
point of potential crisis Hearne bowled Woolley first ball.

Warner's vital problem was now to pin down the late-order
batsmen for the closing overs of the day. One of them was the
captain, Lionel Troughton, a modest performer of no pretence
but of considerable determination; the other was the veteran
Punter Humphreys, a most honourable and experienced all-
rounder who had been one of the solid mainstays of the great
Kent years before the First World War and who was later to
make an honoured name as one of the best School and County
coaches in the business. He was now at the end of his first-class
career (this was in fact his very last match) but nothing could
serve better in a crisis than his long-headed coolness and

reliability. With his captain he began to see the last trying
half hour through; Warner perhaps seeking less for a dismissal
than for run-starvation, feeling that to press too eagerly for a
wicket might be to sacrifice precious runs. Hearne was entirely
to be trusted, though even he was enjoined to stick to off-
breaks and to avoid the possibly loose googly; neither Durston
nor Haig on the day's form could be risked, and for all his
penetrative possibilities Warner did not dare use Stevens.
Harry Lee provided the answer: when steadiness was demanded
he bowled four steady and unproductive overs; and rain ended
the day a little early with 29 runs still wanted and four wickets
still in hand. It may have been some little solace to Warner to
take note that the five Kent batsmen to be involved in the
finish had managed to collect between them in the first
innings the unambitious aggregate of 7 runs.

The odds that night, one would think, were marginally on
Kent; but I doubt whether many rash characters risked their
shirts on either side. It is good to know that there was no
great matter of nail-biting tension; for Warner records that
everyone went off to the theatre to see the 'Old Stagers' –
that amateur dramatic society so closely associated with
Canterbury Weeks and top-brass Club Cricket generally – and
were treated to the pleasurable compliment of a set of topical
verses recited at them amid acclamation from the footlights.
Lovely, lost carefree days and nights – cigar-smoke swirling,
brandy under the belt, a day's play behind you and another
before, the pretty actress flashing her eyes as she patters off
the agreeable doggerel studded with what to her were probably,
unfamiliar names . . .

> O I think I could love you if like Hendren you could pull
> Or like Greville Stevens you could bowl,
> With Jack Hearne and Lee in
> Why, cricket's worth seeing,
> And for Nigel Haig I'd gladly give my soul . . .

A horrid thought strikes the unregenerate reader – were Hendren and Hearne and Lee present? They abode at Lord's, you will remember, in a rabbit-hutch, and Canterbury Week was, as I have noted, Ascot without the horses. It does not matter now, but I hope that Warner, rosily enjoying with his own brand of kindly emotion the last enchantments of his rich career, was able to look round the light-hearted audience and see the whole of his great side enjoying it all too. And after it all – I hope all – went on to supper with the Old Stagers; and Warner very reprehensibly did not get to bed until half-past one, the jingle of cheerful names singing in his head then as in some measure these odd verses, since I read them in Warner's own book when I was nine years old, have rung in mine all my life.

> ... and I lurk round every corner
> For a glimpse of Plum Warner,
> Oh, I'm sure I could love him if I tried.

Trivial words enough, but there is an element in the scene that catches at the vitals. Plum was making his last rounds of his little kingdom; every moment and incident must have held for him, a man of great warmth of response, a poignancy and a regret along with its joy. The company of his great team must have added to the pride and tempered the regret; let these few hours of song stand as symbol for the inexpressible emotions which pervaded, not only that season, but the remainder of his long and honourable years.

The battle was duly joined first thing in the morning: there was perceptible damp on the wicket and the air held flecks of a light drizzle. The ball was wet and Kent should have profited by this; there is no doubt that Troughton and Humphreys were serene and untroubled, and Haig found the ball difficult to hold. Troughton took several confident runs off him, and Warner took him straight off. The hundred went up; Hearne alone kept a staid reliable length, and to the common satisfaction he was turning it appreciably. The crowd was only a few hundred strong, as barely an hour's play could fairly be expected; but among that few hundred a startling tension built itself up. With less than 20 to get, and four wickets still standing, the situation, while still ambiguous, bore a slightly Kentish hue.

Then Troughton, a little over-confident, drove too soon at Hearne's dipper and was caught and bowled. George Wood, the next batsman, was nobody's rabbit – he had opened the innings for Cambridge several times that season – but Hearne on a wet pitch was not greatly to his liking. Humphreys, in no trouble, scored a single here and a two there, but only 6 runs had been added when Hearne beat and bowled Wood and the terrifying margin had narrowed.

The last man but one was Bill Fairservice, sterling bowler for countless years and scorer for even more; he probably remembers these few moments to this very day. For two or three overs he and Humphreys looked like doing the job; a loose ball or two – but Hearne and Durston bowled none – would have seen them relievedly home. Humphreys was placid and unmoved even by a violently confident appeal for a catch at the wicket; Fairservice was brave and willing, but Hearne, now bowling as masterfully as he had bowled all the season, was altogether too much for an unassuming number ten. With the score at 117, six to win, he took a desperate step to get himself away from the danger. He jabbed a ball down on the off-side, saw it travelling slowly, and yelled to Humphreys to run.

Unfortunately he underestimated the capacities of cover-point, who happened to be Hendren; he would have been better advised to try it with any other fielder on the side. Hendren was at it in an eyelid's blink, the ball whanged in to Murrell like a gunshot, and Humphreys, nobly answering the futile call, was stranded a yard or more from home. It is possible that he knew it was hopeless when he started; at any

PATSY HENDREN

Photo:
Sport and General

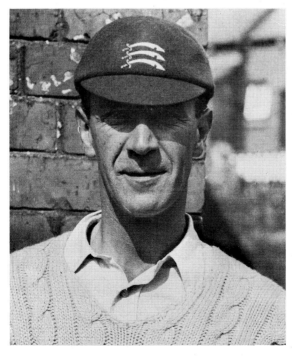

J. W. HEARNE

Photo:
Central Press

Lord's 6.22 p.m., 31st August 1920

Photograph by courtesy of MCC

MIDDLESEX CHAMPION COUNTY 1920

Lee H. K. Longman Durston N. Haig G. T. S. Stevens C. H. L. Skeet
Hearne F. T. Mann P. F. Warner (*captain*) Murrell Hendren

Photograph by courtesy of MCC

Warner at the wicket
Middlesex *v.* Surrey
Lord's, 1920

Photo:
Central News

G. T. S. STEVENS

Photo:
Central Press

rate he came bravely, loyally, characteristically; Fairservice's fatal call ran him out of first-class cricket for ever.

This was the moment; somehow nobody on either side seems to have felt it otherwise. The two balls which Hearne used up to bowl the last man Freeman seem nothing more than a perfunctory necessity. Even Plum himself took a second or two, he says, to realize, when Freeman's bails fell, that Middlesex had actually won, by 5 runs; upon which, he confesses he behaved 'in a most unseemly manner, bounding in the air like a young kangaroo'. ('Blessed if I don't think,' said Sam Weller of Mr. Pickwick, 'as his heart must have been born five-and-twenty year after his body, at least.') Seemly or unseemly, there were few to grudge him his delight, unless it should be noted that Lord Harris, under the press of Kentish emotion, stalked from the ground without a word to anyone, leaving behind him a large basket of cherries destined for a local hospital; which fruit was high-spiritedly commandeered by his lordship's nephew, one N. Haig of the winner's faction, who shared them out magnanimously between victors and vanquished alike. In fairness it should be recorded that there were no other Kent supporters who behaved on this occasion with anything but the warmest generosity; and the congratulations that showered in from all sides did not omit to honour Jack Hearne's supreme performance of 8 for 26 in 17 overs, surely one of the finest sustained and successful efforts of that great and modest cricketer. For after all what a game it had been – a sustained balanced struggle of the toughest and tightest kind, studded with performances of high character and skill – the brave rally of Hendren and Haig, the wily domination of Woolley and Freeman on the openers' pitch, the cool expertise of Hardinge and Seymour, Haig's inspired invasion of Kent's middle batting, Gunasekara's catch, Jack Hearne's accuracy and precision – and, to crown all, the agreeable spectacle of a staid and respectable middle-aged gentleman old enough to know better, cavorting like a young kangaroo.

Score:

MIDDLESEX

H. W. Lee c and b Woolley	4	c Freeman b Woolley	12
H. L. Dales lbw b Freeman	8	b Woolley	11
J. W. Hearne b Woolley	20	lbw b Freeman	10
E. Hendren not out	77	b Freeman	45
P. F. Warner b Freeman	1	c Hubble b Woolley	0
F. T. Mann lbw b Freeman	11	c Seymour b Freeman	0
N. Haig c Woolley b Fairservice	57	b Freeman	0
G. T. S. Stevens lbw b Fairservice	23	lbw b Fairservice	26
H. R. Murrell c Freeman b Woolley	4	b Freeman	16
Dr. C. H. Gunasekara run out	0	not out	4
F. J. Durston b Woolley	1	b Freeman	1
B 1 lb 5	6	lb 1 nb 1	2
	212		**127**

	O	M	R	W	O	M	R	W
Fairservice	22	7	54	2	11	2	35	1
Woolley	27	9	62	4	18	6	42	3
Freeman	14	2	55	3	11.3	3	36	6
Hardinge	7	1	28	0	4	1	12	0
Humphreys	2	0	7	0				

KENT

H. T. W. Hardinge c Dales b Haig	82	lbw b Hearne	16
A. F. Bickmore c Murrell b Dales	8	b Hearne	51
J. Seymour c Hearne b Stevens	73	c Gunasekara b Stevens	7
F. E. Woolley st Murrell b Haig	18	b Hearne	0
J. C. Hubble b Haig	11	b Hearne	0
L. P. Hedges b Haig	10	lbw b Hearne	4
E. Humphreys c Gunasekara b Haig	0	run out	13
L. H. W. Troughton st Murrell b Haig	3	c and b Hearne	12
G. E. C. Wood c and b Hearne	0	b Hearne	3
W. J. Fairservice c Gunasekara b Haig	3	not out	2
A. P. Freeman not out	1	b Hearne	0
B 5 lb 2 nb 1	8	B 4 lb 2 nb 3	9
	217		**117**

	O	M	R	W	O	M	R	W
Durston	17	6	35	0	7	1	30	0
Gunasekara	9	6	11	0				
Hearne	22	2	70	1	16.5	3	26	8
Dales	5	1	20	1				
Stevens	8	1	31	1	4	0	16	1
Lee	3	0	9	0	4	1	10	0
Haig	16.1	8	33	7	7	0	26	0

Middlesex won by 5 runs

Surrey v. Middlesex at the Oval, 7 and 9 August, 1920

There is a sense – actually a precise historical sense – in which a transfer from Canterbury to the Oval is like a walk from a vicarage lawn to a vegetable garden. The ecclesiastical aura is palpably about Canterbury; the Oval itself, far back before modern man emerged from ignorance and lassitude into the admirable specimen he now (I suppose) is, *was* a vegetable garden and no joke intended. It is a great ground, a very great ground indeed; *but*, or perhaps *but* is not the right word, it is a utilitarian and plebeian ground. It smells of beer and the surroundings are damned ugly. Nobody in his right mind would have it otherwise.

Surrey over the generations built a wonderful tradition into this curious oasis. It became, under successive groundsmen and with the essential help of a remarkable succession of outstandingly fine batsmen, one of the greatest rungetting pastures in the history of cricket. In the nineties, in the pre-War slice of our own century, in the nineteen-twenties, Surrey rioted among runs. Abel was nurtured there, and W. W. Read, Brockwell, Tom Hayward. Hayward's quiet and unassuming protégé from Cambridge came there too at his mentor's suggestion, and became one of the two or three acknowledged contestants for the title of the greatest batsman in the history of the game – and fostered in his turn a modest second-string opener who never moved away from his shadow but contrived even in this curious half-obscurity to make over a hundred centuries on his own. The Oval blossomed with runs; in 1920 as in other seasons. Middlesex, appearing there in good spirits after the small-scoring Kent game, must have felt instinctively that it would be as well to tone up the rungetting a little. Kent had been capable enough; but Surrey opened with the world's best batsman, and there were several of his colleagues who could be mentioned not perhaps as in the same class as Jack Hobbs, but certainly not unworthily in the same breath. Only a curious and seemingly chronic shortage of really top-class bowlers withheld them from unchallengable domination; but even without these they were a side of dangerous potenti-alities at all times, were enjoying a cracking good season, and must have seemed to the aspiring men of Middlesex, now committed to a gruelling series of necessary victories, to resemble Apollyon straddling right across the way. And Middlesex men who read further in their fixture lists than the match after next were already uncomfortably aware that Apollyon was going to straddle twice.

A mild counteraction to pessimism was provided by the knowledge that this menacing county had struck a temporary bad patch. They had had such a humiliating leathering from Kent at Blackheath that I doubt if any Surrey supporter ever willingly referred to the match again; and in the match before the present one they had against all the odds of the play permitted themselves to be beaten on the post by Notts. A certain mid-season staleness was perhaps inhibiting them; confidence stumbled, and admitted a new uncertainty; and it was not beyond Warner's practised judgement to assure him-self and his side that whereas Middlesex were by now quite plainly on the up and up, Surrey were shifting perilously towards the down and down.

I am not going to waste words on this match. Middlesex

conducted it as a massacre, and their rivals were systematically dismembered. For the second time in a fortnight Surrey enjoyed, if that is the word, a humiliatingly free third day, as a result of having been conclusively butchered on the second. Because of this, and because this lop-sided cricket match entirely lacked the balanced tensions of the wonderful game at Canterbury, I am regarding it as unnecessary to describe in detail. It would be wrong to conclude that my native Surrey loyalties dictate this reticence; I am by now old enough to know and to do better than that. But nobody will have forgotten that Apollyon straddled twice, and that the second, the final, the crowning encounter more than compensated for the short-comings of the first. Let Surrey retire for the present into the rehabilitating shadows; but meanwhile it would be both shameful and unscholarly to omit further praise of Jack Hearne, whose Canterbury triumph was only a day old, yet who walked primly out to bat five minutes after the start of the Oval match and stayed impeccably at the wicket all day. Skeet assisted him nobly in a second-wicket partnership, and this is of some importance, for this modest success of his at number one confirmed Warner's confidence in the suitability of this good number nine batsman as a partner for Harry Lee. Canny readers whose curiosity has tempted them to flip over the pages to find out what happened in the end will be aware that this inspiration of Warner's brought conspicuously timely success in the future, at his most need.

Hearne's classic 178 needs no latter-day embellishment; it was the perfect exhibition of cool and unassailable correctness. What a treasure this quiet cricketer was – great batsman, great bowler, a great rock of reliability and resource. Greville Stevens' impulsive comment fifty years later is worth record-ing, as he looked back over the miraculous season – 'Hearne was the hero, after Plum'. This is part of the historical per-spective that must be got right; he is no very glamorous or dramatic figure, but his stature is heroic. The Kent game and the Surrey game, the one hard on the heels of the other, proved this beyond any question; especially when we glance at Surrey's second undistinguished innings and observe his analysis – six for 64 in just under fourteen overs. The uncertain weather, trailing light showers about southern England, gingered up the wicket on the second day after Middlesex had batted all the first; Durston made the ball fly about a bit to start with, Hearne demonstrated intellectual and manipulative superiority to finish up with. It was almost as simple as that; almost, I say, because although Surrey perished they did not perish entirely without honour. There were responsible innings from Sandham and Peach, there was aggressive defiance from Fender and Hitch; but the colours that Surrey flew as they foundered were chiefly, and not unexpectedly, centred in two masterly displays by Jack Hobbs. 'Hobbs only made 48 and 60', remarks Stevens a little cryptically, exercising I imagine either an agreeable irony or a pardonable assumption that anything less than a hundred from that batsman was a failure. Hobbs only made 48 and 60, riding the rough weather with the instinctive grace and poise that the memory still so closely cherishes. Even despondent Surrey supporters must have relished being present on that disastrous Monday when their county went down twice, consoled a little in that although they sank, it was not quite without trace. The image of those two polished and high-quality innings must linger with the survivors yet. For the rest, let Middlesex depart with their honours. They deserved them.

Score:

MIDDLESEX

C. H. L. Skeet c Strudwick b Hitch	40
H. W. Lee b Hitch	4
J. W. Hearne c Shepherd b Hitch	178
E. Hendren b Lockton	23
P. F. Warner c Hitch b Fender	2
F. T. Mann lbw b Hobbs	8

N. Haig c Strudwick b Fender   4
G. T. S. Stevens c Hitch b Hobbs   3
H. R. Murrell c Strudwick b Ducat   39
Dr. C. H. Gunasekara not out   35
F. J. Durston b Hitch   14
              B 8 lb 16 nb 3   27
                                      ———
                                       377

	O	M	R	W		O	M	R	W
Hitch	30	10	57	4	Ducat	8	1	19	1
Fender	36	6	143	2	Hobbs	5	1	9	2
Lockton	24	6	59	1	Peach	8	3	12	0
Shepherd	20	7	42	0	Wilkinson	2	0	9	0

SURREY

J. B. Hobbs c and b Hearne	48	lbw b Stevens	60
D. J. Knight c Stevens b Durston	0	c Gunasekara b Durston	3
A. Ducat c Murrell b Durston	5	b Stevens	12
A. Sandham c Murrell b Gunasekara	35	st Murrell b Hearne	5
H. A. Peach lbw b Hearne	31	st Murrell b Hearne	11
P. G. H. Fender c Skeet b Hearne	16	c Gunasekara b Durston	42
C. T. A. Wilkinson b Durston	15	b Hearne	1
T. Shepherd c Murrell b Durston	4	b Hearne	0
J. W. Hitch not out	1	b Hearne	20
J. H. Lockton c Murrell b Durston	1	st Murrell b Hearne	3
H. Strudwick run out	3	not out	17
lb 1 w 1	2	B 7 lb 2	9
	———		———
	161		183

	O	M	R	W	O	M	R	W
Durston	22	4	49	5	13	3	42	2
Haig	4	0	15	0	7	0	19	0
Stevens	11	2	42	0	10	2	32	2
Hearne	13	1	37	3	13.5	1	64	6
Lee	3	1	10	0				
Gunasekara	3.2	1	6	1				

Middlesex won by an innings and 33 runs

Middlesex v. Notts at Lord's, 11, 12 and 13 August, 1920

Warner took his team back across the river in high feather. The Surrey victory had given him immense satisfaction; he praises not only the outstanding batting and bowling performances, but the precise streamlined fielding as well and the neat opportunist catches, Gunasekara and Skeet getting as so often a special note of commendation. He brought back to Lord's a team which not only had great individual capacities at its command but which had in the rigours of its recent away games discovered a wonderful co-ordinated power. I am inclined to think that this resided largely in himself, in his electrifying enthusiasm, his resources of knowledge and experience now responsive to the most immediate demands, and in the love and loyalty that his warm personality extracted, as it were spontaneously now, from the little group of lively and gifted cricketers who had been moving about with him so closely and constantly during the last weeks and months. Like a finely-trained orchestra under an expert conductor, they interpreted his intentions with a superb unison; they and he worked together as if connected to the same nerve-centre. A team like Middlesex in August 1920 polished off all mediocrity with perfunctory professionalism; when matched with rivals of equal power they could bring instinctive skill and improvisation to meet any crisis. Bliss was it in that dawn to be alive, and to be young was very heaven. Wordsworth said this, of course, about something else; but I am sure that Greville Stevens, meditating upon that supreme month, would have said it too, if he could have thought of the words first.

The Notts match was in all significant respects a cake-walk. Here again the tensions did not mount or manifest themselves sufficiently to warrant close or detailed description; let the score-sheet tell its own lucid tale. And on close inspection it contrives to tell quite a lot. You will notice that it bears out refreshingly the truism that I have more than once found it appropriate to utter – that in this first sequence of successes there is wonderful division of labour; if it isn't one man then it's another. This time was Durston's time to come back with a rush; his seven for 79 in the first innings was a fine energetic performance, a sustained strong spell of attack against some of the most reliable batting in England. It wasn't far short of a month since Middlesex had, as an eleven, set foot inside their home ground – the concentration of the prize choice cricket of Public Schools and Universities used to exile them round the outer provinces for weeks at a time in those days – and it was grand to storm back into home territory with such authority and skill. Then again you will see that Hendren took four catches, a routine performance enough it may be but indicative of his vital omnipresence and competence as a fielder; and Murrell stumped two and caught three. Then look at the batting – observe that the Skeet-Lee partnership was a consolidating success, that Stevens made a very useful 61, never letting anyone forget that he was an all-rounder; and that Hendren made 232, his highest score of the season. It is notable that he built this innings as carefully as if it had been the Colosseum; he took 105 minutes over his first fifty, which neither at this or at any other stage of his career was at all typical of this great man's bubbling vivacity. It is even more notable that in the next (and last) 105 minutes of this same innings he added a little matter of 182, repeat 182, driving it would seem largely from half-way down the wicket, battering the Pavilion and Nursery ends alternately with fierce humming punches. In this innings, it was remarked, he used the hook and pull rather less frequently than was his normal habit (which suggests to me that the Notts bowlers bravely pitched the ball up to him, for every schoolboy knew what happened if you dropped one short to Hendren). It was a wonderfully exhilarating display and it signed the match for Middlesex with the gay victorious note to which we are now becoming happily accustomed. Warner himself made 15, his first double-figure

score since Douglas had bowled him at Leyton; and the Notts
second innings was sadly disorganized by none other than
Jack Hearne, who rolled five of them out for 59 in 27 overs,
making all comment superfluous. Nevertheless, I am quite sure
that there was a wise moderation in Warner's mounting
confidence. The bags that they packed that night were labelled
for Bradford; and nobody, least of all this most seasoned of
tacticians, was going to tackle Yorkshire with a careless or
boastful jest on his lips.

Score:

Notts

G. Gunn b Durston	1	st Murrell b Hearne	27
W. Whysall c Hendren b Hearne	96	b Stevens	37
J. Gunn c Hendren b Durston	7	c Murrell b Durston	22
A. W. Carr c Hearne b Durston	61	c Murrell b Durston	23
J. Hardstaff c Hendren b Lee	47	not out	34
W. Payton c Stevens b Durston	12	c Hendren b Hearne	12
S. J. Staples c Murrell b Durston	15	b Lee	3
F. Barratt b Lee	11	b Lee	7
T. Oates c Haig b Durston	6	lbw b Hearne	14
F. C. Matthews b Durston	4	st Murrell b Hearne	13
L. Richmond not out	4	c Stevens b Hearne	4
B 8 lb 5 nb 1	14	B 4 lb 2 nb 1	7
	278		203

	O	M	R	W	O	M	R	W
Durston	36.2	14	79	7	17	3	59	2
Haig	14	5	24	0	8	3	17	0
Stevens	13	2	40	0	5	1	15	1
Hearne	17	2	56	1	27.3	7	59	5
Lee	16	4	47	2	19	4	46	2
Gunasekara	8	2	18	0				

MIDDLESEX

C. H. L. Skeet c Barratt b Matthews	40	b Carr	0
H. W. Lee c G. Gunn b Matthews	41		
J. W. Hearne b Staples	29		
E. Hendren lbw b Richmond	232		
P. F. Warner b Richmond	15		
F. T. Mann c Oates b Barratt	6		
N. Haig b Barratt	2		
G. T. S Stevens c Barratt b J. Gunn	61	not out	10
H. R. Murrell not out	23		
Dr. C. H. Gunasekara did not bat		not out	6
B 3 lb 10 w 2 nb 1	16	nb	1

(8 wkts dec)	465	(1 wkt)	17

F. J. Durston did not bat

	O	M	R	W	O	M	R	W
Barratt	34	8	98	2				
Richmond	35.4	4	125	2				
Matthews	21	4	98	2				
Staples	20	2	92	1				
J. Gunn	9	1	36	1				
Carr					3	1	7	1
Whysall					2.1	0	9	0

Middlesex won by 9 wickets

Yorkshire v. Middlesex at Bradford, 14, 16 and 17 August, 1920

In the perspective of history the nineteen-twenties are clearly seen to belong to Yorkshire by a kind of prescriptive right. Other counties temporarily usurped the Championship leadership, but for how long? Again and again this grimly versatile combination entrenched itself at the top; and even when it didn't, its traditional deployment of concentrated accomplishment, resource, courage, reliability, tenacity, bloody-mindedness and sheer unblinking regional arrogance made this collection of memorable cricketers one of the finest elevens in the variegated history of the game. They were at this moment of time the holders of the title, having deservedly pulled it off in 1919 through greater powers of recovery and, plainly, better cricket than their rivals; and in the weeks at present under our microscope they were lying well up among the leaders. Although not yet the overwhelming formidable bunch who reached their great peak about 1924 and 1925, they contained most of the necessary ingredients – indeed, in this very team that faced Middlesex at Bradford, only Oldroyd, Leyland and Macaulay of the great vintage elevens are missing. For the present David Denton was a welcome but somewhat short-term survival from the pre-war period, and George Hirst was already on the way out, but was of such stimulating potentiality that Yorkshire used him whenever they possibly could. For the rest it is barely necessary to do other than embark upon a sonorous roll-call; everyone who knows the least little bit about twentieth-century English cricket will thrill and quiver to the names as to the sound of massed trumpets – Holmes, Sutcliffe, Roy Kilner, Wilfred Rhodes, Emmott Robinson, Waddington, Dolphin, Rockley Wilson. No great fast bowler perhaps – until the arrival of Bill Bowes, and later of Freddie Trueman, this great county had seemed to be able to manage well enough without – but there was ample compensation in thrustful medium-pacers and swingers, and of course in a rich sample of some of the greatest slow bowling in the world. Add to these attributes the dubious cloudy skies of the North, with background assistance from chimney-vapours, as well as the packed knowledgeable cloth-capped ranks of violently partisan supporters, who reconciled local favouritism with genial generosity in a disconcerting but disarming way – and there would be little surprise if we were to be told that Warner, in what was by now an excitedly determined raid on the Championship, regarded these uncompromising Northerners as far and away his most dangerous opponents.

The fine ground at Park Avenue, Bradford, had taken a
drenching over the recent wayward weeks, and the high-set
pavilion looked down on an ominously green square. Any
vague doubts about the practicability of batting on this kind of
wicket against Wilfred Rhodes, Roy Kilner and all their
quality had no effect on Warner's decision to bat when he won
the toss. He bravely – some would perhaps say rashly – sent
in his openers and prepared to defy the worst. It would perhaps
be an unkind exaggeration to say that the worst, as might
have been expected, arrived fairly quickly; but trouble
happened along, and although no doubt Warner and his well-
tried troops were ready enough to wear it when it came, it did
not make the general task any smoother for that. To begin with,
a spirited fast flier from Waddington struck Skeet between
wind and water in the very early overs and had the effect of
disabling him for the rest of the match; arguably this was
perhaps less of a disaster than if the victim had been Hearne
or Hendren, but it was an unnerving beginning and an
admirable fighter had been rendered useless. Lee and Hearne
courageously mounted a kind of recovery; but the opening
bowlers were soon off and Rhodes and Rockley Wilson were
soon on – the most talented and aggressive left-hand spinner
in the history of cricket at one end, and one of the most
thoughtful, intelligent and accurate right-hand slow bowlers
in the world at the other. On this wicket nothing whatever
could be done to keep out Rhodes; it was the sort of pitch he
cherished and went to bed with; and both Lee and Hearne,
after forging valiantly into the twenties, were variously
deceived, Lee apparently playing too soon and Hearne too
late, if the methods of their dismissal tell a coherent tale at all.
Hendren, bang in form, was unable to do more than snatch a
few hasty singles. Rhodes and Wilson pinned him back on to
his stumps, and the one who broke through in the end and
bowled him for a mere 12 was Rhodes. The innings then fell
calamitously around Warner's ears – almost literally so, for

Warner came in at number five and stayed undefeated to the
end, virtually chained to his crease and quite unable to do
anything but defend. As everybody knows, there was no limit
to Rhodes' capacities at his best; his was the pure wizardry of
his complex art. As for Wilson, he was a scholar and a tactician,
bowling slightly round-arm with a most deceptive flight and
a worrying variation of movement off the pitch. He himself
was known to remark that his most successful ball was the one
which turned from the off when he had meant it to turn from
leg, and as this happy inscrutability was matched by a virtually
infallible capacity to pitch the ball on a sixpence if required,
the concentration needed to stand up to this combination can
be imagined and saluted. Warner did just that; he was in
from the fall of the third wicket until the end of the innings
and he made 8 not out. Haig at the other end burst into sudden
and effective fireworks and made nearly a quarter of his side's
score in a bustle of fours before Wilson bowled him, inevitably;
but by mid-afternoon all was over, 105 had been laboriously
clocked up, and Rhodes emerged with full honours and seven ·
wickets for 53 in 24 overs. Wilson's twenty overs brought him
three wickets only, but he gave away but thirty runs. George
Hirst was not needed at all, and Roy Kilner wheeled his arm
for two maiden overs, nothing more. I cannot help feeling
that Warner deserved all the praise on his own side for holding
the innings so manfully together; but one still wonders
impertinently, fifty years later and a couple of hundred miles
away, why he did not put Yorkshire in.

It is possible that he permitted himself a similar wonder
when Holmes and Sutcliffe took gentle and easy occasion,
while the roller's efforts were still soothing the pitch, to put up
50 for the first wicket. The two great opening batsmen, at the
threshold of their dozen seasons of consistent reliability varied
with brilliance, made the runs at their own pace and in their
own calm and unhurried time. Sensing that, whatever trouble
might still be latent in the wicket, it would still not suit his

fast bowlers, Warner had started straight away with Hearne and Lee, varying the partnership after a few overs by introducing Stevens. This move succeeded; just on tea time the latter delivered one of the worst balls of the season, a slowish long hop on the leg-stump. Sutcliffe, perhaps not yet possessed of all the brassbound inperturbability which was to raise him to classic greatness, hit it straight up into the sky in a very proper endeavour to put it out of the ground, and Middlesex went into tea with one lucky wicket to balance against the disturbing failure of their spinners to extract useful profit from the wicket.

Whether Warner gave them a dressing-down over the tea-cups, or whether the sun started sucking the wet out of the turf again, the tale after tea was quite remarkably different. Hearne and Stevens rehabilitated themselves at once; their spin began to bite and their length steadied; and suddenly York-shire's cool masterful grip slipped and was lost. Holmes followed Sutcliffe with barely a run added; Hearne clean bowled Denton, Roy Kilner mishit Stevens and was caught, and Rhodes and Hirst distinguished themselves by collecting a duck apiece at the hands of the cool unemotional Hearne. Fifty for no wicket was miraculously converted, when Emmott Robinson scraped forward and was stumped, into 69 for 7, all the accredited batsmen gone, the two slow spinners mildly triumphant, and Warner no doubt purring contentedly at point. There seems to have been no occasion whatever, however taxing or bereft of reasonable hope, during these last memorable six weeks of the 1920 season, on which Middlesex were unable to provide a positive and ultimately decisive answer to a challenge.

Late that night and early next morning Yorkshire showed their mettle; they were not the sort of side to be disturbed by a counter-attack. One of the reasons why Yorkshire cricketers are always so successful is that they think their opponents are beneath contempt but always make arrangements to deal with them as if they are not. If Yorkshire's usual batsmen fail, their unusual batsmen resignedly and resolutely take over. In this case Middlesex's destroying run was most effectively and stubbornly halted, at what looked like the last moment or very near it, by the joint determined efforts of the captain and the wicket-keeper.

There seems to have been an amiable tradition for many years that the regular Yorkshire side consisted of ten brilliantly effective professional performers and one amateur figurehead captain, who ignored Wilfred Rhodes' instructions at his very great peril. A learned socio-political thesis could be compiled upon this intriguing practice, which involved an interesting series of charming and unexceptionable personalities who during their terms of office, which were often of comparatively short duration, must have been often felt and expressed a warm and heartfelt sympathy with Daniel in the lions' den. D. C. F. Burton was nominally one of these, but there were abilities and toughnesses latent in this modest cricketer that were ever liable to exhibit themselves in terms of great usefulness – he could dig in and play a sturdy and valuable captain's innings, and he was no negligible fielder either. With the square pugnacious Arthur Dolphin he set himself on this difficult evening to blunt the point of Stevens' and Hearne's successful attack; and this he and his partner valiantly achieved, and more also. The crowd seethed and simmered with appreciation; the batsmen's resolution stiffened; the spinners' momentary advantage was disturbed. Once again, as in the Canterbury game, Warner felt the newly-arrested initiative slipping. Burton watchfully defended, Dolphin moved into attack, the Yorkshire situation was restored, the Middlesex total was passed. Warner tried his fast bowlers, and though neither was immediately effective, they bowled tightly and the scoring-rate slowed. Nevertheless the pair added 80 very important runs, and before Durston bowled him Dolphin had punched his way to an invaluable 52, his highest score of the season and the prime foundation of the substantial lead of 64 which Middlesex had to face when they went in again on the second morning. Hearne finished up with six for 52 in more than 30 overs; his bowling this month was as good as any in his life.

The clouds were still about and the moisture was still freshening up the wicket when hostilities were resumed. This time Middlesex did a little better. Skeet couldn't open, and Hearne for once failed, but Lee improved on his valuable first innings and built a very useful 48 into the fabric of the side's corporate effort. Warner remarks in his account of the game that the second innings was one long struggle, that the wicket was not easy, especially at the end to which Rhodes was bowling (was it ever?) and that for the greater part of the time Yorkshire had the whip hand. It is interesting in the light of these observations to note that even in these adverse conditions Middlesex were able to collect an aggregate of runs considerably higher than any other single innings total in the match. The key to this enigma is surely the tenacity, courage and persistence which were now part of this beautifully co-ordinated team's instinctive resources; as well as partly the central solidity imparted to the innings by Warner's own personal contribution. This amounted to 15 only, and does not look very much on paper; but as in the first innings he nailed himself down and left his partners free to do such scoring as they could. He himself engagingly describes his performance as 'a regular Louis Hall-Barlow-Scotton innings' – it is an endearing and recurring habit of Plum's to draw his cricketing comparisons from forty years back, as if playing to-day he would hark back in similar vein to Maurice Tate or George Duckworth rather than to Alec Bedser or Godfrey Evans; one has to be a little of a cricket historian to cotton briskly on to some of his sly little whimsicalities – it all adds an agreeable and sometimes touching perspective to the slowly-forming picture of this intent devotee. But he played his Louis Hall-

Scotton innings and it gave Hendren and Haig with their more youthful energies the freedom of any looser bowling that might happen to be offered them, and both these batsmen snapped up this opportunity gladly. Hendren in particular played a fine commanding innings, making free even with Rhodes, and certainly savaging Waddington for all he was worth. Only Rockley Wilson, wheeling them in with his own determined accuracy, defied any batsman to score readily off him at all; and it was Wilson who eventually moved one from leg, whether intentionally or not he no doubt deliberately failed to specify, and Hendren's thick edge was most gloriously snapped up by Waddington in the slips, snatching the ball right-handed (he was a left-hander) as he tumbled headlong. Only a few moments later he did precisely the same thing to dismiss Mann ('our Bonnor', says Plum engagingly) for the second half of a pair of spectacles, a mishap which that good-humoured batsman no doubt refused to allow to depress him unduly; and Nigel Haig appeared to play what Greville Stevens has recently described as the most important innings of his life. He played, as we know, plenty of these, and how reassured Warner must have felt so often that season when Haig's lean, wiry, light-stepping figure with the slightly bow-legged loping walk came on to the field to bat, so often in circumstances which in any other side or at any other time might have been called critical. On this occasion he decided straight away to play, as he termed it, swashbuckle; and swashbuckle he did, all over Park Avenue and its surroundings, peppering the stands with courageous lofty drives and paying as little respect as possible to Wilson and Rhodes. It was from Haig, and earlier from Hendren, that most of the runs off Rhodes came; as for Wilson, so few runs were scored off him anyway that it is clear that even Haig in his inspired frenzy was unable to do more than extract a few token runs from this quizzical and exacting schoolmaster.

Here Yorkshire found themselves unhappily at a dis-

advantage. Roy Kilner, who normally bowled second fiddle
to Rhodes – and what a second fiddle! – and who would have
been invaluable both in his own right and as a relief if and when
Rhodes tired, had gone down with stomach trouble and did
not appear again for several days (a young colt named Leyland
was called upon to deputize for him, and played his first game
for Yorkshire in the following match). This left the two
veteran slow bowlers to carry on as best they could with little
relief – George Hirst bowled a few tidy overs but did not
penetrate – and Haig took his life in his hands and hit them.
They dropped him at mid-off and they dropped him in the
deep; but before Rhodes, as he was bound to, bowled him
and restored his own self-respect, he had made 86 hugely
satisfying runs and taken the side's total well past the 200 mark.
Stevens and Murrell, building happily on these earlier achievements, added of their plenty a handy 21 and 13 respectively;
and although he does not say so, I do not see that Warner
could have felt anything but satisfied with the total that his
team had amassed. Loyally they had all contributed; even
Skeet had hobbled in to hold his bat there while his partner
scraped as many runs as could be gathered in; and Yorkshire
were at least set 198 to win, which made it, in the sight of
reason, anybody's game. And before passing on let us pause to
salute the no doubt weary but satisfied Wilson, whose 44
overs had yielded but 62 runs. Half these patient overs, half,
were maidens; and he had collected six wickets in the course
of this supremely patient and unrelaxing war of aggressive
attrition.

Yorkshire had the whole day to get the runs in; the dimension of Time was accordingly removed from their complex
worries. It is to be greatly regretted, of course, that Roy
Kilner was removed too; there were therefore only nine
wickets to fall and the previous two days' cricket had knocked
the top off the rich green surface. Yorkshire knew better than
anyone else what the dangers were: and they philosophically

noted and checked off the first of their misfortunes when Durston, very soon after the start, ran one away from Sutcliffe's bat and Hendren took the catch in the slips. Holmes and Denton batted calmly enough for a while, but Holmes sparred like Sutcliffe at Durston and it went through comfortably to Murrell; and when Warner changed the bowling once the shine went off, Hearne got the dangerous Denton lbw and Hirst drove too soon at Stevens and got no further than the impervious Mann at mid-off. Burton pushed himself up the order and came in to join Wilfred Rhodes, who had seen his way through potential crises of this kind several hundred times in his career already, and was to see a tidy lot more before he gave up, and these two settled without apparent difficulty and were together at lunch time with the side's total somewhere in the eighties.

There were still about 120 runs needed, and the four wickets down had to be counted as five; Middlesex savoured this as another rare opportunity to snatch their advantage – this was the sort of situation that the last tingling weeks had begun to accustom them to, and there can have been no lack of optimism at the lunch-table. And the lunch did Durston good. Rhodes and Burton were as careful and confident after as before, but Durston came back at the pavilion end with a refreshed and breezy antagonism. He had the wily Rhodes on to his back foot, cagily watching him on to the bat until the last instant; and in the first rasping overs he twisted one back on to the splice at an awkward angle and Rhodes cocked it dangerously in the air. Warner at point, keen as an eight-year-old, raced in with hands outstretched for the catch; he had the ball between them for one delirious moment, and then his knee jerked it out again. Warner's dash carried him face to face with the square-leg umpire; and no doubt that impassive official had never seen in all his life so agonizedly disappointed a face so closely confronting his own. Common humanity compels the narrator to hasten mercifully to the quick sequel; Durston

clean bowled Rhodes in the same over, and all was serenity
once more. Only a few moments later he got rid of Burton
too, and an even calmer serenity descended; it is painful even
for conjecture and hypothesis to contemplate the self-excori-
ating agony which would otherwise have ravaged Warner
had not providence, and Durston, provided speedy compensation for his failure to make the catch.

Burton was out with the score at 120, and for a time Emmott
Robinson and Dolphin showed the same kind of aggressive
purpose that had seen Yorkshire to first innings points on the,
second day. But Haig succeeded in getting his only wicket of
the match when Hendren snapped up Robinson; and to
Warner's own double pleasure and relief he himself took a
catch when Hearne deceived Dolphin into mishitting an off-
break. And at this point the score-board showed eight wickets
down for 140, Yorkshire 57 runs behind, Kilner absent ill, and
the presiding fairies of Middlesex apparently rubbing their
hands preparatory to the now familiar round of victory
applause. With the rapid fall of the wickets after lunch
Middlesex might be pardoned for a feeling of rapidly mounting
euphoria; and one member of the side, cheerfully strolling up
to Warner at the fall of the most recent wicket, was ill-advised
enough to remark happily to his captain, 'Now we've got
them, sir.' This, according to Stevens, produced an unexpected
explosion of anger from one who was otherwise the incarnation
of sweetness and light, and the offender was glad to lose
himself in an engulfing humiliation in the outfield until the
terror was passed.

He had plenty of time to consider his *faux pas* and even to
forget it; for Warner's instinct could not have been surer. At
the moment when the rebuke was being administered, the last
batsman making his way to the wicket was the capable and
belligerent Abe Waddington, a character of spirit and aggression rather than of diplomatic compromise, a fire-eater whose
valour outweighed his discretion and whom Horatius would

have been happy to have welcomed among his bridge-holding
reserves. His partner was the watchful Rockley Wilson, with
ages of lore and experience behind his amused eyelids, who had
given up batting to concentrate on bowling, but who had in
his time made several first-class centuries and knew all the
arts of batting several times over and was able at a pinch to put
the majority of them into practice. Waddington, himself,
in his day not far off greatness as a bowler, was no slouch as a
batsman – he too made at least one first-class hundred and I
would guess that worse batsmen than he have gone in at
number seven for England. It is therefore entirely under-
standable that Warner should have seen fit to insert the flea
in the ear of his rash fieldsman; and Wilson and Waddington,
playing up and down the line with the greatest coolness and
confidence, proceeded to justify his action almost up to the hilt.

This was stern unyielding stuff; quite possibly the toughest
crunch which Middlesex met in this grinding Odyssey of
theirs. Durston and Hearne, set in their several rhythms, were
bowling with their tails up when this last pair began their long
haul; it was not long before the unexpectedly confident
batsmanship put their tails down. Warner rang a few changes,
none of them markedly successful. Haig came on for a few
overs, but was ineffective and came off again; Durston came
back. Hearne at the other end did not abate his meticulous
length and accuracy. Once he thought he had Waddington
conclusively lbw but the umpire did not agree; later Wilson
played at him and missed and nobody on the ground knew
how it failed to hit the wicket. The runs came ticking up;
the 53 that was this last pair's target dwindled to 30, then to 20.
The crowd hummed and swayed with excitement; the
cricketers felt they were playing in an encircling ring of
electrified steel. Every run got its roar of applause.

There was a sudden appeal for stumping; Waddington had
gone forward to Hearne and missed. Murrell had the bails off
in no time, and Stevens at short leg would have given it out,

but didn't happen to be the umpire. 17 now to win; Warner, not for the first time, talked absorbedly with Murrell and Hendren. Hearne was bowling superbly but was clearly tiring; did he dare replace him with Stevens, who gave the ball more air and often gave away a four or two before he settled to a length? Warner later thought that he may have left Stevens too late; he had bowled a few overs before lunch and removed Hirst, but since then Hearne and Durston had provided such an effective combination that his recall would have seemed premature. Now at last Warner made up his mind; and with the most earnest and heartfelt instructions to give nothing away, he handed the ball to Stevens and left the rest to him.

Stevens and Durston bowled in dead unearthly silence. When the ball was hit, the roar came; if runs accrued, the roar was redoubled. They bowled as tight as they knew; the batsmen watched with immense concentration, scoring a single or a two here and there, playing dead-batted, tensed, but completely controlled. This was surely the finest cricket of Warner's fine season, a marvellously-endowed fielding and bowling side menaced by the courage and determined skill of two late-order batsmen hell-bound for snatched victory. Durston's rhythm did not break; Stevens, only nineteen remember, a wrist-spinner, a high-spirited adventurous youth, disciplined his bursting talents to a most admirable control. The runs ticked up, the tension was hard to bear; it was difficult to know which was worse, the dead silence as the bowler ran up, or the unnatural liberated yells as the batsmen played the ball away. Warner must have bowled every ball in his mind as Stevens ran up and bowled it in person, willing it to drop on a length. Once Waddington let out at a half-volley and drove it smack into the stumps at the far end – a bit of jam for Middlesex, for it would have been at least one run.

Only five to win and this deadly silence as Stevens began

his next over – no sound but his feet as he ran up, and that
lightly enough. For four balls that over Waddington played
stern and straight, bang in the bat's middle, as trim as a number
one batsman, as reliable as the Town Hall. The Yorkshire
crowd bayed and vociferated their delight; the hum died, as
customarily, as the bowler turned at the end of his not very
long run, the silence fell, as customarily, as he took the first
step towards his fifth delivery. At this crucial moment a character in the crowd delivered into the dead silence one compact
sentence in a superb Yorkshire accent, a statement of high
complacent certitude. 'You're beat, Ploom!'

That did it, says Stevens; he had invoked the gods. I am
disposed to agree with this, for the dramatic tensions were
crackling so palpably about the scene that any disturbance
whatever violated the proprieties and deserved instant retribu-
tion. In this case it came pat. Whether the cry impelled Stevens
to a variation of pace, or infinitesimally disturbed the batsman's
concentration, no one can say; but Stevens let loose an unexpectedly fast off-break and it knocked Waddington's middle
stump out of the ground. Middlesex had won by 4 runs, and
I am sure that the fierce pressure on Warner's nerves gave him
no residual energy or desire to spring in the air like a young
kangaroo. According to Stevens, this manoeuvre was duly
executed by Haig; and they all got off the field in a daze, and
were met most magnanimously in the pavilion by congratu-
latory Yorkshiremen, who prefer to win as a rule but who
could not on this occasion have been more disarmingly
friendly. The social scene became relaxed and fragmentary;
and Stevens signalled the occasion by draining uninvited the
first whisky and soda of his life, an especially large one ordered
by Frank Mann for his own consumption and temporarily
left unwatched. It is reassuring to know that Mann was, as
might have been expected, magnanimous about this. Everyone
in Middlesex could be magnanimous on that day. They had
just, by marginally superior performance, won, at a crucial

moment of their season's progress, one of the greatest cricket matches ever played.

And while we are on the subject of magnanimity, I would like to help to ensure the perpetuation into cricket history of the joint performance of Wilson and Waddington. It can do these two men little good now – they are years dead, both of them, as are so many in this chronicle; but it does cricket and cricketers good to be reminded from time to time of performances like these. I rate this stand of Wilson and Waddington as the greatest single passage of this greatest of Warner's seasons. I am sure that the survivors of this match, players and spectators alike, as well as us who merely read about it, and perhaps in admiration write about it, will never quite forget it, or the two fine players whom to remember it is to honour as they deserve.

Plum, says Stevens, was a little overcome by the situation and said some very nice things to all his team. I should have felt that the nice things would have been said whether he was overcome or not; he himself said that the finish (as well it might) tried him more than any other that season. He at least retained his self-command sufficiently to warn them against reaction; it must have been a sobering thought that after that epic struggle they had to travel to Lord's to meet Somerset on the very next morning.

Score:

MIDDLESEX

C. H. L. Skeet c Waddington b Rhodes	1	not out	0
H. W. Lee c and b Rhodes	21	c and b Rhodes	48
J. W. Hearne lbw b Rhodes	26	c Hirst b Wilson	9
E. Hendren b Rhodes	12	c Waddington b Wilson	56
P. F. Warner not out	8	lbw b Wilson	15
F. T. Mann c Burton b Wilson	0	c Waddington b Wilson	0
N. Haig b Wilson	25	b Rhodes	86
G. T. S. Stevens lbw b Rhodes	5	b Wilson	21

P.W.—8

H. K. Longman c Burton b Wilson	1	b Waddington	3
H. R. Murrell c Robinson b Rhodes	2	c Rhodes b Wilson	13
F. J. Durston c Waddington b Rhodes	2	lbw b Rhodes	0
B	2	B 4 lb 5 w 1	10

105   261

	O	M	R	W	O	M	R	W
Waddington	11	6	11	0	26	8	61	1
Robinson	5	2	9	0	7	0	28	0
Rhodes	23.4	6	53	7	41.5	9	98	3
Wilson	20	11	30	3	44	22	62	6
Kilner	2	2	0	0				
Hirst					5	3	2	0

YORKSHIRE

P. Holmes c Hearne b Stevens	22	c Murrell b Durston	13
H. Sutcliffe c Hearne b Stevens	23	c Hendren b Durston	2
D. Denton b Hearne	1	lbw b Hearne	21
R. Kilner c Durston b Stevens	7	absent ill	0
W. Rhodes c Hendren b Hearne	0	b Durston	26
G. H. Hirst b Hearne	0	c Mann b Stevens	11
E. Robinson st Murrell b Hearne	2	c Hendren b Haig	10
D. C. F. Burton b Hearne	36	b Durston	19
A. Dolphin b Durston	52	c Warner b Hearne	15
E. R. Wilson lbw b Hearne	4	not out	39
A. Waddington not out	1	b Stevens	25
B 16 lb 2 w 1 nb 2	21	B 3 lb 4 w 3 nb 2	12

169   193

	O	M	R	W	O	M	R	W
Hearne	32.4	13	52	6	26	6	48	2
Lee	4	0	20	0				
Stevens	19	2	43	3	6.5	2	17	2
Haig	5	2	8	0	9	2	30	1
Durston	13	5	25	1	32	8	86	4

Middlesex won by 4 runs

Middlesex v. Somerset at Lord's, 18, 19 and 20 August, 1920

It was perhaps as well for Middlesex that Somerset provided them with what in all charity must be called an easy fixture on their return from Bradford; it would have been likely that had they been immediately faced with Kent or Surrey (and fixtures with these were still to come) they might have cracked under the pressure. As it was they were doubly fortunate, for the wayward weather came south with them, and the first day's play was considerably interrupted by rain. This is infuriating enough, and in this particular context it no doubt did not escape Warner's lively mind that they only had to draw a game to render their Championship chances as near null and void as made no odds; but it did give hard-driven bowlers and fielders, who had also had the additional diversion of a train journey from Bradford, the chance of a little longer rest than they might otherwise have been able to snatch.

In the previous game the odd number nine batsman who always seemed to lurk on the fringe of this otherwise compact eleven had been H. K. Longman, one of the military brotherhood and an old Etonian of no great pretensions, who benefited considerably from Warner's amiable practice of filling in at the last moment with one of his old friends. At this stage of time it is puzzling to the chronicler how Warner's ultra-keen and circumspect cricket mind could have been content, in the particular prolonged crisis under review, to admit mediocrity if better material were available. It can only be concluded that better material was *not* available; and I only raise the point because it is a curious one which would not now be permitted to arise, and because it not only puzzled the comparatively untutored chronicler but also the highly authoritative and experienced Greville Stevens. This is not urged in disparagement of Longman, an excellent cricketer by any standards other than the toughest, but is partly introduced now because he is to be fairly regularly in the side until the great culmination

and will be featured in the standard team photograph at the
end of the royal road. It is also by way of a farewell to the
colleague of his who did replace him for the Somerset match
and is then lost to our view for good – the mercurial Gunasekara, the dark lightning-flash from Ceylon, whom I have
frequently had to notice and commend in the early and even
later stages of this celebrated progress. Gunasekara bows out
and is lost; I somehow wish that he, perhaps above any of the
similar number nines who capriciously came and went that
season, could have shared more openly and publicly in the
final rejoicings. No doubt he enthused with the rest, and was
most certainly not forgotten by Plum; but I give him my
personal salute now, in the Somerset match in which he made
3 not out, was not put on to bowl, and, I have no doubt
whatever, fielded like a wizard.

Otherwise the Middlesex side was unchanged. I am a trifle
exercised about Skeet, who was too crippled to stand up in
the second innings at Bradford, but who was able to walk out
fit and fine to field at Lord's the day, or at most two days,
afterwards. Perhaps the long train journey shook him back into
shape; there he was at all events, as active and as effective as
life, and caught a catch in his usual impeccable style to get
rid of M. D. Lyon. True, he got a duck when he batted, but
plenty of entirely undisabled men do this regularly; in the
second innings he helped win the game with a steady 22 not
out. I do not concern myself any more about Skeet's health;
from now on he is unobtrusively though nobody knows it,
not even himself, preparing for a tidy immortality.

Let me be fair to Somerset in this match; the result looks a
walk-over but the match was not of this kind at all. On the
first day they weathered awkward rainstorms and some
nastily accurate bowling by Hearne (who else?), and Durston;
there were good runs from John Daniell, an elegant little
innings by that admirable batsman Jack MacBryan, and 58
from one J. A. S. Jackson, whose name does not ring very

resonantly in the historic corridors of cricket but who for all that stood manfully in the breaches this day and deserved well of his county. He seems to have played for Somerset in this one season only, making one century and doing very reasonably well, but sinking without trace at the end of it and never even rating an entry in *Wisden*'s Births and Deaths columns, into which so many curious nonentities have strayed. Here he is at any rate in one of his few but honourable moments of success. I hope I can ensure that he does not go unrecorded for ever.

Somerset reached 210, not without credit, the wicket never being easy and the bowling, as we cannot help recognizing, in full and destructive practice. When Middlesex went in on the second day a few preliminary overs were bowled by R. C. Robertson-Glasgow, no less (would he had recorded his impressions at length . . .) before the cunning of the great Jack White began systematically to probe the Middlesex defences at one end, with the tried accuracies of Bridges and the case-hardened professional Robson deployed at the other. Skeet departed, Lee departed, in a sudden dismaying crumble Hendren and Haig departed. For a few testing overs an equilibrium was maintained only by the most watchful of skills. Fortunately for Middlesex Jack Hearne was in cool command; and this was one of those occasions, not very regularly experienced but noted loyally by all who write about this cricketer, when he proved that it was a characteristic of him to force the pace in a manner quite unlike his own should the state of the game demand it. As a rule he played serenely, demurely, avoiding agitation; at these specialized times, and this appears to have been one of them, he came out and attacked as if he had been Hendren himself, driving and cutting with a most exhilarating freedom. Frank Mann, whose form of late had escaped him altogether, retrieved it with some genial hitting; and Warner, who was also mighty short of batting practice, went in lower down than usual and indulged, when the edge had been knocked off the far from negligible Somerset attack, in an agreeable partnership with Stevens that helped to put a rather rocky innings on its legs again. They topped Somerset's total but only just; and Warner declared next morning only 8 ahead.

The wicket was drying irregularly and had all the happy ingredients of a hell-brew. Warner virtually left it to Hearne and Stevens; he knew he was safe. There is no point in detailing the collapse, for Somerset subsided with barely a groan. The wiseheaded Braund, in his last season, put careful bat to ball as he had been doing to such effect all his life, but he knew and they all knew that he and the others were fighting the tide. Hearne buzzed and spun from one end in this his great destroying month: Stevens flighted and spun from the other. Haig picked up the odd wicket or two, including the vital one of Braund, and Somerset were cleaned up and cleaned out for 90 and there was nothing for Middlesex to do but go carefully for victory. Three wickets went down, but there was nothing to it; they could enjoy a few more hours' rest before turning their faces to the provinces again.

Score:

SOMERSET

J. Daniell c Murrell b Hearne	22	b Stevens	3
J. C. W. MacBryan b Stevens	23	st Murrell b Stevens	10
M. P. Bajana lbw b Hearne	6	c Stevens b Haig	0
J. A. S. Jackson b Durston	58	c Murrell b Hearne	6
F. A. Waldock b Lee	17	b Stevens	13
M. D. Lyon c Skeet b Durston	35	c and b Hearne	4
L. C. Braund lbw b Hearne	12	b Haig	18
J. C. White b Stevens	15	lbw b Hearne	1
E. Robson c Stevens b Hearne	1	c Stevens b Hearne	11
J. J. Bridges lbw b Stevens	1	not out	10
R. C. Robertson-Glasgow not out	4	b Hearne	3
B 8 lb 7 nb 1	16	B 6 lb 4 nb 1	11
	——		——
	210		90

	O	M	R	W	O	M	R	W
Durston	20	4	58	2				
Haig	4	I	II	0	5	0	16	2
Stevens	19	2	55	3	15	3	35	3
Hearne	20	5	37	4	20.I	6	28	5
Lee	18	5	33	I				

MIDDLESEX

C. H. L. Skeet c White b Robson	0	not out	22
H. W. Lee c Robson b White	13	b Bridges	21
J. W. Hearne lbw b White	66	b Bridges	2
E. Hendren c MacBryan b Robson	5	b Robson	25
N. Haig c Braund b Bridges	9	not out	10
F. T. Mann b Bridges	30		
G. T. S. Stevens c Robertson-Glasgow			
b White	33		
P. F. Warner b Bridges	28		
H. R. Murrell st Lyon b White	12		
Dr. C. H. Gunasekara not out	3		
B 18 lb I	19	B	5
	———		———
(9 wkst dec)	218	(3 wkts)	85

F. J. Durston did not bat

	O	M	R	W	O	M	R	W
Robertson-								
Glasgow	5	I	16	0	2.4	I	6	0
Robson	21	8	57	2	7	3	14	I
White	44	13	91	4	13	3	29	0
Bridges	25	9	35	3	16	6	31	2

Middlesex won by 7 wickets

Warwickshire v. Middlesex at Birmingham, 21, 23 and 24 August, 1920

The result of the Somerset match put Middlesex on top of the Championship for the very first time. On top by the fraction of a point only – 72.94 to Lancashire's 72.50 and Yorkshire's

72.38; but on top. They knew quite well that there was to be
no relaxation for them whatever; Lancashire, their nearest
rivals, had a fortunate run of easy fixtures to finish up with,
in the course of which they were going to play two games
against Worcestershire who had not won a match since the
first week in June, and who weren't going to win any more
and never looked like it; and Middlesex were still bearing in
mind the encouraging prophecy of the friendly journalist at
Leyton that to win the title they would need to win every one
of their remaining games. I have tried to show already how
comparatively craggy and rough-obstacled was the path
Middlesex were obliged to tread, and what reserves of courage
and strength every single member of the team had had at one
time or another (and some at many different times) to draw on
to make the task good. When they came to Birmingham for
what they must now have eagerly marked down as their very
last match but two, it must have been with mingled enjoyment,
relief, resolution and (somewhere at the back of all their minds)
a resigned and pervasive weariness forced off by an iron
resolution. This wonderful parade of victories may look like a
triumphal procession; I am sure that there were moments
when it more closely resembled, to those involved in it, a
barefoot march on nails.

Warwickshire, however, were not as tough a proposition
as they would have been before the war, when Frank Foster's
wonderful youthful panache had seen them to the top of the
table. Foster was unhappily a wartime casualty and the county
was having a struggle. Tiger Smith was an England wicket-
keeper; Willie Quaife triumphed by technique and character
over diminutive height and increasing age as few batsmen
(and bowlers) have been able to do; the new post-war captain,
the Honourable Freddie Calthorpe, was just beginning his
most active and valuable period of captaincy during which his
batting, his bowling and his invigorating personality all played
a vivid part in his county's regeneration; and, in the stocky

Harry Howell, Warwickshire had what was reputed to be the fastest bowler in England. There was character and experience and talent and potentiality there, but not a combination; it is difficult to think that Warwickshire went into this match with any great hopes. Courage of heart in plenty, no doubt, but not much more.

At the very beginning of the game Haig ripped a sizeable hole in the batting, Calthorpe and Charlesworth going for nought each. Quaife and the stylish Len Bates stemmed the early fury for a while, and in fact saw Durston off; but in this month of miracles nobody seemed proof against Hearne, who collected three wickets on the trot as soon as the gallant little partnership was broken. There was some valiant batting towards the end of the order, when Haig's initial freshness had worn off with the shine – they took quite a number of runs off him as his length and pace declined; and the contributions of genial amateurs like Waddy, Fiddian-Green and Rotherham made a very sickly score-board look very much better-complexioned. It is very unlikely, however, that the final total of 186 caused Warner, as he came off the field at the end of the innings, any very serious worries. His congratulations to Hearne, who took 5 for 54 in 18 overs, cannot have helped seeming almost routine in quality by now, so regular and so generous were that player's invaluable services in these last weeks; but I hope he held a little warmth in reserve, for he was about to need it.

Middlesex made none too good a start. At one end they had to adjust themselves to Harry Howell's considerable pace; at the other Calthorpe exercised his vigorous talent for swinging the new ball most disconcertingly. The earlier batsmen found difficulty in settling, and Calthorpe forced both Skeet and Lee to injudicious strokes. Worse still, Hendren was beaten at once; these three batsmen were all out before the score was 30, and Calthorpe bagged them all. The shine was still on, the two bowlers were unremittingly energetic, the innings trembled.

That it did not do more was due to Plum Warner; at long last, after weeks of tentative play in which the loss of personal touch was I imagine disregarded in the happier context of his team's more general success, he experienced the satisfaction of contributing once more the full quota of his skill as well as his encouragement and experience. And at the other end Jack Hearne, as if he had not offered his weight and more also a score of times over already, proceeded to play what must have been his finest innings even of this season of all seasons. Against Warner's stubborn discrimination and Hearne's cool timed skill all Calthorpe's spirited vigour and Howell's destructive pace broke unavailing. In an hour the initiative had been completely, finally transferred.

It was the decisive partnership. Warner's 45 was of far higher value than the mere count of runs. When he got out the Warwickshire total was in sight; and Mann came cheerfully in and obliterated it. He and Hearne added 171 in very quick time indeed. It must have been almost as pleasant for Warner as for Mann himself to watch his vice-captain's controlled aggression show so effectively and decisively at last. He had had a patchy season, something less than representative of his best, and he had long been in the background while vital work was distributed among others, abating nothing of his keenness and good humour the while. Now he watched Hearne's delicate finesse extract the sting from the bowling at the other end, while he crushed it from the other. It comes back to me now, after all of fifty years, that only a few months later a school friend of mine from Coventry, nearly ten years old, described to me with glowing delight what must have been this very innings. Hearne's matured artistry at the other end naturally left less impression on him; what he remembered, and communicated his memory so well that I, writing now in 1970, remember his heightened pleasure as he spoke of it (and he was a Warwickshire supporter, too), was Mann's commanding aggression, his wonderful driving, his power.

Howell and Calthorpe could do nothing with him, nor could any of the other accredited or non-accredited bowlers that Calthorpe hopefully, and later hopelessly, tried. He gave the whole of the assiduous but indifferent Warwickshire attack the father and mother of a leathering; and Hearne at the other end, skilful and delicate, scored almost run for run with him without anyone but the connoisseurs noticing him at all. Mann got out unluckily nine short of his hundred; Hearne proceeded calmly to his double century while Haig and Stevens had a pleasant knock-about with the change bowlers. When Warner declared, Hearne's model innings had lasted nearly five hours, a beautiful 215 not out to top off his bowling performance. A lead of 234 was a healthy asset; it gave Middlesex a chance to feel that Fate and Opportunity were for once not breathing stertorously down their necks.

As often happens at such times, Warwickshire rallied in their second innings. There can never have been a shred of a chance of their winning – their early wickets, though they did not fall so early or so rapidly as they had done in their first attempt, were not prolific enough for sanguine hopes to arise. But this time, and it is almost a relief to chronicle it, Hearne was ineffective. He was no doubt mildly tired – nobody could have expected more achievement from him than he had so richly provided already; but not only was Hearne ineffective but Stevens and Durston were both on the expensive side, and the batsmen were allowed a freedom that they had not previously enjoyed. Willie Quaife, neat, compact, light-footed and classical, produced a delicate gem of an innings of 61 in nearly three hours, one of his own quiet and contemplative performances without ostentation or superfluity. His was the keystone of an admirable communal effort – and he had lively amateur backing from Waddy, Fiddian-Green and Holdsworth, all admirable untensed innings played, one imagines, for sheer enjoyment rather than for any possibility of a favourable result. Tiger Smith, an excellent batsman to be going in as low as number nine, hit hard and effectively too; and the cheerful hitter Rotherham, going flat out for a six off Harry Lee, was quite marvellously caught by Skeet in the outfield off the highest hit that Warner remembered seeing anyone make. Skeet made a habit of punctuating this sequence of matches with dazzling little fielding episodes of his own; this is one that has been preserved through time by the instant impression that it made, and still retains its power to fascinate from afar.

Middlesex only had 50 to get and collected them almost absent-mindedly. Calthorpe got rid of Lee, but the rest was routine. Middlesex already knew that there could be no let-up yet, for Lancashire had thrashed Worcester in two days and were already on the triumphant move to Leyton for their next game. Yorkshire, surprisingly beaten by Surrey at the Oval, dropped back. The main rivalry continued until the end.

Score:

WARWICKSHIRE

L. A. Bates c Hendren b Hearne	22	st Murrell b Stevens	12
Hon. F. S. G. Calthorpe c Murrell b Haig	0	b Durston	16
C. Charlesworth b Haig	0	lbw b Stevens	18
W. G. Quaife lbw b Stevens	29	c Mann b Lee	61
R. L. Holdsworth b Hearne	0	c Hendren b Durston	32
Commander C. F. Cowan lbw b Hearne	5	c Murrell b Durston	10
Rev. E. F. Waddy c Durston b Haig	40	b Tanner	43
C. A. Fiddian-Green c Hendren b Hearne	21	c Hendren b Tanner	35
E. J. Smith c Mann b Haig	19	not out	39
G. A. Rotherham lbw b Hearne	41	c Skeet b Lee	3
H. Howell not out	4	run out	2
B 3 lb 2	5	B 8 lb 3 nb 1	12
	186		283

	O	M	R	W	O	M	R	W
Durston	9	3	22	0	23	1	81	3
Haig	22	5	84	4	4	1	17	0
Hearne	18.1	4	54	5	10	3	23	0
Stevens	5	1	21	1	24	5	82	2
Tanner					18	8	35	2
Lee					12	2	33	2

MIDDLESEX

C. H. L. Skeet c Smith b Calthorpe	3	not out	18
H. W. Lee c Fiddian-Green		c Charlesworth	
b Calthorpe	9	b Calthorpe	5
J. W. Hearne not out	215		
E. Hendren c Rotherham b Calthorpe	3	not out	23
P. F. Warner b Quaife	45		
F. T. Mann b Rotherham	91		
N. Haig b Fiddian-Green	14		
G. T. S. Stevens not out	17		
B 18 lb 3 w 1 nb 1	23	B 4 w 1	5
(6 wkts dec)	420	(1 wkt)	51

A. R. Tanner, H. R. Murrell and F. J. Durston did not bat.

	O	M	R	W	O	M	R	W
Howell	28	4	84	0	9	4	27	0
Calthorpe	28	1	82	3	9	5	12	1
Rotherham	20	1	90	1				
Quaife	21	3	91	1				
Charlesworth	1	0	3	0				
Bates	1	0	12	0				
Fiddian-Green	5	0	28	1	1	1	0	0
Cowan	3	1	7	0				
Holdsworth					1.1	0	7	0

Middlesex won by 9 wickets

Middlesex v. Kent at Lord's, 25, 26 and 27 August, 1920

Kent came to Lord's over the dead bodies of many vanquished counties; but their record was not unblemished, they had

permitted Surrey to avenge the Blackheath murder, and they
were not serious Championship contenders. Nevertheless the
memory of the damned close-run thing at Canterbury still
brought smooth Middlesex flesh out in goose-pimples, and it
was still no doubt a matter of interested conjecture as to what
kind of mood Lord Harris might be in when he met them
again. Middlesex, riding the high waves of providential good
fortune, which in its own fashion is so often a reward for hard
striving, were nevertheless very coolly and realistically
conscious of the potential menace in this opposition, and were
also screwed several points tighter themselves towards a
tension which was becoming a degree or two more unnatural
than was healthy. Let us be as realistic as we can, of course;
these were for the most part young and uncomplicated men,
not unduly given to high nervous pressures, enjoying this
young man's carefree game in the prolonged sunlight; tension
or no tension, it disturbed no pulse-beats or digestions, though
it might make a good or even enthralling story when once
over and done with. Yet Warner, for one, a high-strung,
tender-hearted, rather emotional man, as he appears in his
writing and his own account of himself, was not only a potential subject for nervous twitterings but was himself not young
and not robust. I wonder if this electric season lost him any
sleep? Putting myself, now, in his place, then, I do not see
how terrifying nervous anguish can have been avoided; by
the Kent match I for one would have been wishing, with deep
Falstaffian fervour, that it were bedtime and all well.

Whatever the stresses may have been, Middlesex as a team
gave very few indications of being troubled by them. They
batted first on a hard true wicket (Warner no doubt congratu-
lating himself on the luck of the toss, which postponed the
arrival at the crease of a Frank Woolley whose last innings had
been 133) and against an opening attack that had guile rather
than penetration, Skeet and Lee built a nice level commodious
foundation to the innings. They saw the openers off quite

composedly and it was perhaps a little disappointing that
Skeet should have touched Freeman to the wicket-keeper just
when he was beginning to produce a stroke or two; and it was
more than disappointing, it was actually seriously disturbing,
when Freeman immediately disposed of Hearne for a duck.
There was no panic and no collapse; but Lee was back in the
pavilion before the hundred was on the board, and a glance
at the completed score-sheet will indicate at once that anything
might have happened to the middle and later batting had the
next defences given way. Accordingly it is right to say out
boldly at this stage that the next and, as it turned out, virtually
last defences of this innings resided in the staunch and vital
partnership between Warner himself and Hendren, and that
it may be said, without anybody knowing it at the time, to
have won the match for Middlesex.

It cannot have escaped the notice of anyone reading this
account with any eye for personal fortunes at all that Warner
himself had had no very successful batting season. He had made
the early hundred against Sussex, and had played brave
innings worth many times more – notably against Essex in that
exhausting rearguard battle against Johnny Douglas in which
hero stood up against hero like a confrontation in the *Iliad* –
but there had been strings of small scores to balance these, and
nobody knew about batting consistency and the desperate
efforts to recapture it better than this man. Yet he never seems
to have allowed the natural despondencies attendant upon
personal failure to put any kind of brake upon his ramping
enthusiasm and his delight in the gratifying corporate successes
of his side; through all these crucial games he moved as one in
committed authority, pulling every ounce as much of weight
in his county's progressive victories as if he had himself made
the runs or taken the wickets which his vigorous encouragement
and shrewdness were enabling his team to do without his
substantial aid. How satisfying then, for both himself and the
county, when at the time of greatest need he could play his

part with them so effectively again; his innings of 67 this day must have glowed in his own mind as brightly as it was enjoyed and approved by his fellows and supporters. At the other end, of course, Hendren directed the attack in person in one of the finest of his great innings that season. This one was a classic; he took no risks except those inherent in his brilliant attacking methods, but he used his feet with rare rapidity against Woolley and Freeman and did what he liked, wherever he liked, with the others. Freeman in particular, never an economical bowler, was given a powerful bashing which might have discouraged a lesser spirit; and no bowler in the end had the satisfaction of his wicket, for, after four hours of busy aggression, he miscalculated and was run out, and apart from a hit or two from Joe Murrell the innings simply dribbled away. Nevertheless, 379 was a very comfortable total to have on the board, and Warner and Hendren, who supplied between them nearly two-thirds of this total and a very considerably higher proportion than that of the communal morale, must have felt not for the first time that they had deserved conspicuously well of their county. Freeman, grinning his way back to the pavilion with six wickets against his name, whether they cost 158 runs or whether they didn't, must have felt with some sense of fulfilment that he had done so too.

Kent began on the wrong foot by losing Wally Hardinge at once, and for a time it looked as if Seymour and Woolley in their turn would successfully play out for Kent precisely the kind of role that Warner and Hendren had played for Middlesex. Seymour's elegance and determination at one end balanced Woolley's fluent imperial genius at the other – and, Jack Hobbs apart, Middlesex met during this kaleidoscopic Odyssey no greater or more commanding batsman than the Kent left-hander. The panorama of the last ten crucial games includes virtually a comprehensive line-up of the toughest, most talented, highest-gifted, most distinctively-endowed players in the land, and they all made runs and took wickets, they all exhibited their high graces in what looks in retrospect one of the most prolonged and successful final grand benefit performances in the history of public entertainment. Plum Warner, avid for their failures with a part of his mind, must have somehow delighted at the very same time in their adorning successes; in none more than this innings of Frank Woolley's, this glorious upstanding batsman of free-flowing beauty of execution. He has not happened to say so, in print at any rate; but I cannot think that Woolley's 96 at Lord's can fail to have been one of the highlights in his life's memories of a series of cricket matches he never forgot till he died.

As it happened, Woolley found little substantial support; for Hearne cut short the dangerous early partnership by inducing Seymour to give a catch, and the middle batting splintered about his ears. The only other batsman to shoulder like responsibility was that other tall left-hander Johnstone, less talented of course but not a scrap less determined; and Warner had to draw on all his bowling resources before the two were got rid of. Stevens, after getting two quick wickets in the middle of the innings, was rather positively mastered, which perhaps may not be surprising if we remember his age, which was nineteen, and Woolley's experience, which was, to say the least, comprehensive. Haig was only sparingly used, which suggests to the absent chronicler that he was having one of his uninspired and directionless days; and neither Hearne nor Durston could seem to do much more than contain their men. Harry Lee, oddly perhaps, picked more plums out of the pudding than anyone, bowling unassumingly bang on a length and tempting not merely Johnstone but the great Woolley himself to untimely indiscretion in the end. His modest breakthrough must have gladdened Warner's heart, now no doubt beginning to flutter a little unnaturally at all signs of crisis or frustrating absences thereof; and his three wickets for 29 in ten overs were a powerful contributory cause of the healthy

lead of 147. Middlesex would have been happy no doubt to
enforce a follow-on here, but Freeman and Fairservice got
effectively in their way; and by now, half-way through the
second day, it was the task of the home county to lay on the
wood as powerfully as possible so as to give Kent an over-
powering task in the fourth innings while leaving time enough
to get them out.

They were, of course, in a happy position; but nobody,
least of all Plum Warner, would have been fool enough to take
things lightly with Kent's potential in mind. They hadn't
only Woolley to reckon with; Hardinge and Seymour were
in the first rank of county batsmen that year, and huddled down
in the middle order was some very powerful University talent,
Bickmore and J. L. Bryan, and Johnstone, who had already
shown his quality. Middlesex could not afford to waste runs
or time; they had to get on and get them quickly. They lost
Skeet early, and Lee and Hearne took some little time to root
themselves. No doubt they were in very little danger of bog-
ging themselves down, and in the light of the subsequent
history of the first-class game it is quite surprising, not to say
exhilarating, to realize how quickly Jack Hearne for one was
able to score while appearing to the unwatchful eye to be
perfectly stationary; but on this occasion it would seem that
the orders to crowd on the pace were, however willingly
jumped to, never quite satisfactorily implemented until the
bustling arrival at the wicket, twinkling-footed and pugnacious,
of the belligerent Hendren, full of subversive energy. This he
proceeded to deploy all over Lord's in the ensuing three-
quarters of an hour by loosing on the brittle Kent attack a
bewildering onslaught of a quite devastating order. He was
here, there and everywhere all at once; his creased cap perched
anyhow on his head, his sleeves rolled half-way up and half-
way down, his amused Irish grin savouring and no doubt
commenting on the unfolding situation, he was down the
wicket at the flighted spinners, back on his stumps for the

shorter-pitched, prompt with the cut and the square slash, with the full-powered hook off anything not of a full length, but also this time with drives fanning from extra-cover to deep mid-wicket – and no bowlers spared, but Freeman and Fairservice his favourites, with a few luscious wallopings off Wally Hardinge inserted for fun. *Wisden* says he batted for fifty minutes, Warner says forty; whichever is correct, the score while he was in sky-rocketed by 107, of which he collected 84, including thirteen boundaries and a six. 'It will never be forgotten', said Warner, 'by those who were at Lord's that day' – and to some of us who were not, but who were happy to see Hendren hustle in later years, the thought of this superb display of virtuosity can even kindle in imagination an ineffaceable memory of an experience almost as vivid to them as if they really had been there. A pity, perhaps, that he could not have ridden on the crest of inspiration to his second century in the match; but he was to do this four times in his career, and we may restrain our tears of regret.

Hearne and Lee had performed with considerable distinction, and Haig, in the common rush for runs, collected a cheerful 37, but all the other batsmen sacrificed themselves bravely in the stampede. Warner himself, feeling it perhaps undignified to let his back hair down like the rest (and the metaphor is as inappropriate as it could possibly be) did not bother to bat himself; he was content to declare, sitting on the top of a pile of runs, setting Kent the fearful total of 416 with nearly all day to get them in.

Impossible? No, of course not. Improbable is the more accurate adjective; but Warner knew what he was about in ensuring that it was as tough a task as could be. His bowlers had had a gruelling season, and during the last three weeks they had been driven to the extremes – willingly driven, indeed, but flesh and blood are apt to remind their possessor that he ignores their limitations at his peril. With the last vital match now only twenty-four hours away, Warner dared not overtax

his stock bowlers – it is noticeable that in this very game Haig
bowled 17 overs only, and there was a certain reliance on the
journeyman Lee – but as against that he could not optimist-
ically expect all Woolley's companions to leave him on his
own a second time. There is no indication that he was ever
afraid that Kent would make the 416; but I can feel it legitimate
to guess that he felt a considerable lightening at the heart as
the successive wickets fell.

Nobody has left much of an account of this match. Warner
refers with relish to Hendren's innings, Stevens gives little
more than the score; it was part of the run-in to the great
climax, all chroniclers want it out of the way. I sympathize
with them; their mouths, like mine at this moment, water for
the joy of the contest to which all events in this astonishing
season appear but the prelude. Nevertheless, it was not a
perfunctory match at all, and the two sides saw to it that the
Friday afternoon was not a frivolous waste of time. I doubt if
Kent at their most sanguine ever thought it was really on; but
they paid their conquering opponents the compliment of
behaving from the first as if they fully intended to get the runs.
And it ought, I think, to be made clear that it would not have
been a monstrosity if they had, given their great talent. It
needed Hardinge and Seymour, say, to have made 80 or 90
each and Woolley to have made 150 – none of these things
were at all out of the ordinary – and after that there would
have been a bare 100 runs to have been dealt between Bryan,
Bickmore and Johnstone, cracking a tiring attack. On paper
it's simple. If Warner had qualmish moments he no doubt
spent them doing just such melancholy arithmetic.

Of course it didn't turn out like that, but it could have.
Luckily Durston's stamina was unimpaired; this tall broad
smiling companionable man bowled with a tireless vigour
upon which Warner must have rested as against a protective
wall. What is more, he bowled tight; and the fact that he
picked up no early quick wickets did not seem to discourage

him in the slightest degree. This time Wally Hardinge settled down and looked menacing; and at the other end the admirable Seymour performed unobtrusively and effectively the elegant role that he played in so many of Kent's games that season – that of the entirely dependable and graceful second string. When Stevens at last drew Hardinge up the wicket and Murrell stumped him, Seymour quite happily transferred his allegiance to Woolley, who gave every indication, as he leaned with that incomparable languid fluency into the bowling, that he was carrying on where he had been compelled to leave off in the first innings. The latent aggressiveness that his immense charm concealed was in this innings loosed quite severely upon Hearne, who for once found his accuracy and composure a little fretted at the edges; and the Kent batting cruised happily and steadily down the sunny afternoon, less like a lost cause than an agreeable gala outing. At one mildly worrying point they were nearly 200 for 3; and this was not Warner's idea at all.

It was the gigantic Durston who broke it all up. Seymour's meritorious 76 was cut off short when Stevens took a catch in the gully, and it was Durston too who ran one through to trap Woolley lbw when the left-hander had eased his way to 44 and was no doubt harbouring plans for a second fifty to be built upon his first. It must have been about this time that any phantasmagoric Kent hopes faded without pain or strain into the air above St. John's Wood; and, although there was nothing whatever in the nature of a collapse, there was no further stand of substance to build on the impressive foundation. Hubble the wicket-keeper, half-way to being a wicket-keeper batsman of the characteristic Kentish stamp (Ames–Evans–Knott) put up a sturdy fight; Bryan and Bickmore, the University batsmen of promise and performance, sketched elegant and effective proposals for innings of character without being allowed time to develop them at any length. Bickmore had come to the match happy from his first hundred for Kent; Bryan, a punishing left-hander of such distinction that he later won a place on an Australian tour, had made over 50 in the innings of Bickmore's success; they lacked but experience, and perhaps a more realistically attainable target. Stevens clean bowled Bryan, and Durston found the edge of Bickmore's bat – after that there were failures, and the edifice of the Kent innings, so carefully and easily designed, began to be loud with creaking and cracking noises. Durston and Stevens saw to it that equilibrium was not regained; they were held up for a while by Fairservice, laying about him with relish as a kind of personal compensation for his sad error of judgement at the end of the Canterbury match of thrilling memory, but it was a genial gesture merely and they found it simpler to let him get on with it and remove his partners. This they did with competence and despatch, and an hour before the scheduled end Middlesex ran out victors by 153 runs.

Durston had bowled 30 overs for 74 runs, one of his finest sustained performances of the whole season. The score-sheet printed in *Wisden* shows him the destroyer of Seymour, Woolley, Hubble, Bickmore and the captain, Troughton, which makes five according to my calculations; the bowling analysis disconcertingly credits him with four only. Similarly Stevens, noted as having got out Hardinge, Bryan and Freeman only, gets four chalked up to him in the analysis. Small matter after all these years; small matter after ten minutes, actually; but I have given Durston 5 for 74 in my version, and this gives him seven in the match, a most admirable return at the end of a crackingly hard season.

Warner and his men went back up the Pavilion steps – or at least, some of them did; the others made their seemly exit to the rabbit-hutch 75 yards away – knowing that they had won eight matches in a glorious row. For the moment the satisfaction of success piled on cumulative success must have been exhilaratingly sweet; and no doubt the secondary inconvenience of reckoning up points and percentages was euphorically postponed until such moments when heads might be guaranteed to be a little clearer. The news came through in the course of the last afternoon that Lancashire, their closest and most severely menacing rival, had dusted Essex off their hands at Leyton with the greatest possible ease, and were even then packing jubilantly to return northwards where they were to play their last match against Worcester, a confident cake-walk against a county whose return to the Championship that year was amiably described by *Wisden* as a 'complete failure'. It was accordingly only too obvious to the assessors of Middlesex's chances both in and out of the dressing-room that there was no sense in allowing for anything but a thumping Lancashire victory; and this was an admirable thing, for it left no cowardly loopholes – everything must be staked on winning the last match, the whole team must go into the field with no other idea. For the present – that is, for the Friday evening of 27 August – they could accept the generous Kent congratulations and survey with momentary pride the gruelling climb that they had achieved together. Tomorrow was to be, very conspicuously, another day.

Score:

MIDDLESEX

C. H. L. Skeet c Hubble b Freeman	29	lbw b Woolley	6
H. W. Lee c Seymour b Woolley	46	lbw b Hardinge	44
J. W. Hearne lbw b Freeman	0	lbw b Fairservice	67
E. Hendren run out	170	b Fairservice	84
P. F. Warner c Fairservice b Freeman	67		
F. T. Mann c Bickmore b Hardinge	13	c Hubble b Collins	4
N. Haig b Freeman	4	b Freeman	37
G. T. S. Stevens b Freeman	1	st Hubble b Woolley	9
H. K. Longman c Woolley b Freeman	3	st Hubble b Freeman	0
H. R. Murrell not out	25	not out	4
F. J. Durston c Johnstone b Woolley	12		
B 7 lb 1 w 1	9	B 10 lb 3	13
	379	(8 wkts dec)	268

	O	M	R	W	O	M	R	W
Collins	10	1	36	0	6	0	36	1
Woolley	30.5	6	63	2	12	3	38	2
Freeman	44	7	158	6	13.2	2	71	2
Fairservice	19	1	57	0	18	3	71	2
Bryan	4	0	20	0				
Hardinge	13	3	36	1	7	1	39	1

KENT

H. T. W. Hardinge c Murrell b Haig	1	st Murrell b Stevens	32
G. C. Collins lbw b Durston	13	c Stevens b Hearne	8
J. Seymour c Durston b Hearne	28	c Stevens b Durston	76
F. E. Woolley c Longman b Lee	96	lbw b Durston	44
J. C. Hubble b Stevens	13	c Lee b Durston	25
J. L. Bryan b Hearne	0	b Stevens	20
A. F. Bickmore c Durston b Stevens	2	c Murrell b Durston	19
C. P. Johnstone c Hendren b Lee	41	b Hearne	2
L. H. W. Troughton c Haig b Lee	0	b Durston	1
W. J. Fairservice not out	11	not out	21
A. P. Freeman b Durston	4	b Stevens	0
B 13 lb 9 nb 1	23	B 10 lb 2 w 1 nb 1	14
	232		262

	O	M	R	W	O	M	R	W
Durston	24	3	64	2	30	10	74	5
Haig	8	2	21	1	9	3	22	0
Hearne	21	4	45	2	21	3	68	2
Lee	10	2	29	3	13	3	23	0
Stevens	12	0	50	2	14	1	64	3

Middlesex won by 153 runs

6)   *The Crown*

Middlesex v. Surrey at Lord's, 28, 30 and 31 August, 1920

So it was come at last, the supreme confrontation; the obstacle
that had strenuously to be surmounted were the unbelievable
success to be made real; the last match of the season, known
and appreciated as such of course before ever the first ball was
bowled in early May, but not right up to the very day before
it started invested with all the enormous pressures implied in
the crucial battle that it was going to be. The tensions that
surrounded it were born of a hundred incalculable accidents of
Championship pointage and percentage dotted unnoticed
through the long panorama of the summer; only fortuitously,
through some failure of Lancashire's batting at Whitsuntide
in Bradford, some unaccountable collapse by Yorkshire at
Maidstone, a flash at the Oval of Surrey's opportunist brilliance,
a touch of genius here and there in some match-winning
individual, Wilfred Rhodes or Johnny Douglas, Jack Hobbs or
Frank Woolley – only by chance, under sun and shower and
the infuriating incalculabilities of lost form, had this contest
suddenly become vital, symbolic, a key to the delight or the

disenchantment of a mixed brand of men welded so happily
into a coherent intricate whole, a crown (or not) on the lifetime's achievement of one of the most dedicated and committed of all cricketers, who found now by the happiest of all
chances that his personal and his public goal were identical
and that in his last culminating effort he would have behind
him, almost palpably, the warm goodwill and encouragement
of the whole of the cricketing world.

It was settled then; Middlesex had to win. Lancashire on
their home turf flexed their muscles for the easy coast home,
all but finally convinced that they were on to a certainty.
With no ill-will in the world they rooted unashamedly and
hopefully for Middlesex's opponents. Middlesex for their part
contemplated these opponents with mixed feelings. They
remembered, and no doubt called it to mind monotonously,
regularly, for therapeutic refreshment, that when they had last
met those opponents on their opponents' ground they had
given these opponents one of the sharpest hidings of their lives.
Heartening the recollection, indeed; yet Middlesex in this
testing and variegated season had matured not only into self-
knowledge but into a wholly healthy respect for any opponents
that she might meet. Plum Warner by this time was not only
the captain of his team; he was almost by instinct and by
intuition the conscience and the consciousness of his team as
well, and under-estimation of opponents was never one of his
failings. It was one of his outstanding qualities, this generous
capacity to recognize and to proclaim an opponent's virtues,
and by now his whole team shared his instinctive responses.
Therefore under all the happy reminiscences of the great Oval
massacre that no doubt enlivened the dressing-room or rooms
during the last bright days of that August of fifty years ago
there cannot help but have run a cool restrained note of
warning. In some ways Warner would rather have had any
opponent but Surrey for this most testing match of his lifetime. Apollyon may have been beaten off at the Oval, but here

he was again straddling very aggressively and menacingly at Lord's.

Surrey we have met before, but we recognized them only perfunctorily, knowing that the last cross-roads would provide a more leisured moment for the encounter. They were now at the fruitful beginning of a remarkable period in their history – a period in which they would beat any side in the Championship without anyone being surprised in the least, but in which they never won the Championship or for more than a short spell or two ever looked like doing so. The reason for this is almost too obvious to detail – their tremendously strong batting resources were never adequately matched by comparable bowling. The Oval wicket, as I have already noted, was as hard as a brick, being constructed primarily of the tombstones of aspiring bowlers who had broken their hearts on it; and a very rudimentary knowledge of cricket history is enough to show that Championships do not come the way of counties who cannot get the other side out twice. Between the times of Richardson and Lockwood in the fast-receding past and of Bedser, Laker and Lock in the entirely unforeseeable future, Surrey took Championship honours only once, in 1914, and the grim sardonic humour of its opponents' partisans has commented that that was the prime cause of the outbreak of the First World War.

In 1920 they were sustaining themselves very well in the upper reaches of the table, but the pattern that was to obtain for so many seasons in the twenties was already beginning to emerge – a slightly less than adequate handful of bowlers were being adroitly manipulated into the semblance of a formidable attack by a very clever captain who himself provided three parts of the variety in his own lively person. Percy Fender, who was now virtually in complete charge of the eleven, having quietly taken over from C. T. A. Wilkinson at the latter's request late in the season, was about to emerge upon the twenties as the greatest unrecognized captain of the decade –

an honour to pass in due time and succession to Beverley Lyon and Brian Sellers – and was already as batsman, bowler, fielder and ubiquitous intelligence a very fearsome proposition for an opposing captain, needing all Warner's sagacity to combat. He had with him a highly talented but erratic medium-paced seam bowler in the individualistic Tom Rushby, a somewhat moody and sardonic character of independent temper, given, says Stevens, to wearing black socks, and the hugely popular and thrustful fast bowler Bill Hitch, of whom my own experience taught me that he always promised more than he fulfilled but that he was such a vigorous and engaging fellow that he left behind him no enduring sense of disappointment. To back these he had the medium swingers of Gillie Reay, a tall leathery bespectacled warrior who did immense damage in London club cricket but who never had the time to establish his real talents very firmly in the regular first-class game – and that, save for Fender's own multifarious wiles, which included virtually the whole bag of tricks, was about the lot. No great equipment for Championship contenders, it would seem; but it should not be overlooked that the Surrey fielding was perhaps the best in the country at the time, and that their batting during the twenties – in 1920 it was only just beginning to consolidate – was of almost Olympian quality. It led off – there is no harm in reminding ourselves – with the greatest professional batsman that England ever possessed, and it carried on with the other half of one of his immortal partnerships; and the season before had seen the brilliant success of the cool and lovely stylist D. J. Knight. Add to these the names of Ducat and Shepherd, Fender himself, Jeacocke and Peach, and the sure foundation of the truest wicket to bat on in the kingdom, and you can gauge the potentiality of this county's scoring power at once. In this season they had had a disappointment with Knight, who came late into the side, found difficulty in picking up his form, and then received a savage crack on the temple off the meat of Maurice Tate's bat while fielding at close short leg, a mishap which lost him to the eleven for the rest of the season, and it seems crippled his full flow of confidence for ever. The one advantage that may be said to have accrued, however, from this distressing accident was the final and undisputed establishment of Andrew Sandham as Jack Hobb's opening partner. This is not the time or place to enlarge on the value of this incalculable benefit; but even in this very brief chronicle the worth of this great player, in his proper position at the proper time, will be evident enough, as it was evident to Middlesex over the last two crucial days.

This variously talented side arrived at Lord's in the best of health and spirits, with the heart's blood of Northamptonshire dripping from their jaws. While Middlesex had been busy using up valuable physical resources dealing with Kent, their friends across the river had enjoyed an agreeable spell of batting practice in the Midlands, where they had achieved a total of 619 for 5, to which Jack Hobbs had contributed 3. There is no need to go into the gargantuan details beyond remarking that towards the end of this astonishing orgy Percy Fender made 100 in 35 minutes. It should be noted, however, that whether Surrey intended it or not, Northants made over 300 in each innings (430 in the second) and that the bowlers upon whom Surrey relied for success were treated without politeness or reserve. I am prepared to bet that Plum Warner took care to read all about this in the morning paper, and that he may even have made an amiable comment upon it to Percy Fender when he met him on the great day. Even the slightest hint of a latent vulnerability was a valuable asset at this moment.

The Middlesex eleven lined up for the crucial struggle was the same as had beaten Kent. I have hinted before at the vaguely unusual characteristic of Warner's teams this season; they seem almost literally to have consisted of ten men and a dog – or if not a dog, an odd man out, a batsman going in number nine and not bowling, a friendly passenger. I have noted the fluctuations of identity through the season; for the last match or two Harry Longman had been the fortunate one, and Harry Longman it was who took his place with the team to-day. I have already recorded a mild surprise that Warner, with the mightiest crunch of the century on his hands, could afford to carry a comparative lightweight into this crucial game; but he did, and the enigma remains.

For the rest, the team was the splendidly-equipped machine that we have grown to know and to live with over the crowded strenuous weeks. Middlesex did assuredly owe something to good luck this season – not a single one of her key players missed a match, or, as far as I can trace, a minute, through illness or injury. No muscles were slipped, no bones were broken, no feverish colds were contracted. Some benevolent angel must have been detailed to keep watch, with a particularly vigilant eye on behalf of the brittle and vulnerable Hearne. He or she did his or her job to a nicety. Middlesex had to call on 18 players only that year; two of these played in no more than a match or two, while seven were in every single fixture. Haig missed one game only, and Stevens was a regular after the 'Varsity match. Familiarity, usage, friendship, loyalty, custom, co-ordination, all played their part in shaping these happy companions into a superb striking force, above all, leadership, generalship even – Joe Murrell nicknamed Warner 'The General' early in the season, and it somehow stuck – generated an affection and a co-operative energetic goodwill that made up for all light-weight discrepancies as well as enhanced many times over the ostensible aggregate of the many personal talents involved.

'It may be imagined', says Warner in his reminiscences, 'with what tense feelings I looked forward to the match.' It may indeed; some flesh and blood I know of could not have stood it, and while Warner's spirit was indestructible his solider substance was on the frail side. 'We were all a little on edge', says Stevens. Let these two authoritative understatements suffice. The cumulation upon Warner's nervous system of all these concentrated crises – the chance of an eighth win, the chance of the snatched Championship, the allied but quite separate tensions induced by the fact that this would be his very last match, his very last after all those crowded unforgettable years, the delivery of a piece of himself into the shadows – would have inhibited many lesser men into quivering incapability. One can only envy him in this as in other respects, and try to enjoy his unusual experience at second hand.

And at second hand it must be – cannot help being. To anyone well versed in cricket history and legend, the game is a classic of its kind, perpetuated through Warner's own account of it into a glamorous legend all on its own. Any narrative attempted now, however originally or freshly phrased, must necessarily lean heavily on Warner's version. Stevens has recently added some invaluable comments, but they can only be footnotes to the prime tale. An outsider coming late to it is necessarily handicapped; but he can do what Warner and Stevens could not, and that is realize the spectacle objectively, at a distance, in relation to all the other surrounding factors – the time, the place, the occasion, the characters, the skills, the emotions of this, that or the other participant – as no involved person could ever do. How to do it without destroying the essence, that essence of high tension communicated by Warner, and without too slavishly running with Warner's committed narrative, that is the problem.

Mercifully for all, the morning of Saturday 28 August was fine and bright. Warner, writing only a few months later, recalls it as a little cold, though the sun must have come through quite powerfully later, as none of the fieldsmen in the photograph taken that day wore sweaters. Stevens fifty years later simply says 'it was a lovely day'. I am sure it was, or to his youthful enthusiasm felt like it; and if there were any deficiencies in the weather, they were amply made up for by the exhilarating excitement of the London crowds. Middlesex

enthusiasts had had all their incentives progressively sharpened
for them in the mounting delights of the last weeks; they
thronged in on that Saturday like a football mob. As for
Surrey, they brought their supporters in across the river in
swarms. 'Hard-benched, straw-hatted, glad, ingenuous crowds'
–wasn't that how the poem went? – in they packed, that fine
bright August morning, their spirits high and the war over.
Stevens saw them as he came, five deep up the St. John's
Wood road as far as he could see, a chattering, hustling,
excited company over which eagerness and excitement
trembled and quivered like a heat-haze – a barely precedented
sight for a county match and not often bettered since for a Test.
These crowds, remember, had not had a Test to watch in this
country since 1912, they were starved and craving for the big
occasion; and here was a big occasion offered them, not by
label, but by quality of performers and happy accident of
circumstance, all symbolized with unusual felicity in the
personality of the central figure whose farewell it was to be and
whose triumph they were praying it would be as well. The
feelings of Surrey supporters would have been bewilderingly
mixed; a lifelong Surrey supporter myself, I was a little too
young to be there and a little too young to identify myself
with the complex situation. Nowadays it would be different;
if I had been the age then that I am now, I hope that I should
have had sufficient romantic generosity not to have grudged
him a victory if it came. Clamorous and joyful, the crowd
packed itself into the illustrious ground.

Lord's then had a barer look than it has now. The Pavilion
was much the same and so was the Mound Stand; but the
spectators at the Nursery End were accommodated with a few
limited rows at ground level only, under flat awnings, and the
then Grand Stand was rudimentary compared with the present
ornate object over which Father Time so impassively swings.
It is a foolish truism, in this context, to add that there was no
Warner stand either (although in a strange metaphysical sense

it might be argued that the foundation stone of that future building was in a measure laid during these three very days). There were mere spaces where there are now populous stands – at least they *can* be populous, I wish they were so oftener – and the seating capacity was far less generous than it is now. But the gaunt black chimney behind the Mound Stand belched generous black smoke then as it does now; and the Pavilion imposed then, as it imposes to-day, upon the strangely hushed and cloistered square of turf perhaps the most awesome embodiment of authority and dignity in the whole universe of sport. Nowadays about 35,000 spectators can be crammed in at a pinch; in those days it was equipped perhaps for 30,000 at the most; and Warner estimates that when he walked out to toss with Fender there must have been 20,000 there already.

'We were all a little on edge' – Stevens' bald statement must stand for an indescribable complex of tensions. Warner alleged that he felt quite calm all through – no doubt once the procedure had got under way his great experience quietened any jumps and kept him serene. Stevens found himself a shade irritated by perfect strangers button-holing him; there was a kind of buzzing electricity in the air. The amateurs on the pavilion balcony watching 'the General' go out for the last time to toss must have felt, perhaps imperceptibly, an upsurge of affection along with the common anticipatory keenness. If the professionals, craning their necks awkwardly out of the remote rabbit-hutch, also watched him go, I have no doubt they felt the same, perhaps more so – they had done him so proud that season, those five. Amateur and professional alike, they went into this match and played it as much for him as for the county or themselves; and the great undertow of hum from the packed benches and the volume of the applauding roars when they came, made it clear that the crowd was with them and with him too.

Warner won the toss, as he so often did; the accustomed Middlesex ranks went almost automatically into their so

familiar routines. It was just such a commonplace manoeuvre
as had happened on so many other Saturdays like it – the bell
ringing, the spectators settling to their day's watch, the
umpires emerging; a roar for the fielding side, the amateurs
coming down the centre gangway, the knotted cluster of pro's
converging on them from the hutch; then behind them the two
batsmen to another roar, advancing side by side to where the
opposing fast bowler, flexing his shoulders, was purposefully
making for his run's end. As the welcoming applause engulfed
Skeet and Lee, and the crowd suddenly seemed overwhelming
and the players very small and lonely, did Warner give himself
time to think that this thing, in these terms, that had happened
so often before that it was almost mechanical, was happening
now for the very last time in his life?

Surrey were handicapped by no such tensions. The Lord's
wicket on the first morning of a match has always been
favourable to a lively and energetic fast bowler who can use
the seam, and Bill Hitch on his day could generate great pace,
accompanied generally, it is related, by a very fearsome
involuntary grunt at the moment of delivery. Tom Rushby
at the other end, however eccentric his black socks made him
appear, had accuracy and considerable control over variations
in flight; the new ball in the hands of these practised attackers
had to be watched with intense care. It is perhaps not to be
wondered at that Middlesex found themselves stepping gingerly
at the start; and the relatively inexperienced Skeet got an
early edge off Rushby and was caught in the slips. The reassuring sight of Hearne's impeccably straight bat partnered
by the defiant crouch of the solid and accomplished Lee gave
Middlesex supporters, as well as team-mates, easy breath for a
while after this first set-back. They dug in watchfully, turning
a single here, dabbing another there, for the most part refusing
to be tempted, eyeing the swing and avoiding it, putting
confident defensive bats when needed to combat straight
good length, composedly setting themselves as they so often

had done together in the past and would do in the future, to see away the shine and the first penetrative aggression before beginning to think about the serious business of run-making. As they dug in, the crowd continued to pour through the gates; the police began letting them through in lavish numbers to sit on the grass.

All of a sudden Hearne misjudged one of the first of his forcing shots; he stopped in the middle of a pull, and Hitch, following up his run, caught and bowled him. And the shock of this disappointment was hardly past its first bitterness and Hendren had barely announced himself with a scurried single or so, when Fender, who had enterprisingly brought himself on as an early first change, induced Lee to aim adventurously through the leg-side field and Bill Hitch at short leg took the blinder of a lifetime one-handed, one of his specials, and three Middlesex wickets were gone for only 35 runs.

It was dramatically appropriate that Plum Warner in his crowning match should have to come in to a crisis. And crisis it was; another wicket, and Middlesex would be struggling badly against a whooping swooping team all tasting blood and victory, bowlers stimulated by early success to unsuspected reserves of aggression, fielders avid for the catch and trigger-happy for the destroying throw. Warner came in through the deafening welcome to a friendly but bristling opposition, and as he took guard he must have summoned up to his aid all his ordered and sorted stores of experience and courage, for this was a time when they were all going to be needed, all of them.

After the first anguished minutes the game stabilized itself. Warner relied entirely upon a well-tried defensive technique, leaving the runs to Hendren. Little question now of Patsy repeating his orgiastic performance of two days ago – all that was in a happy hey-day as alien as if it had been in another season or another country; to-day the struggle.

Runs, said Warner, were terribly hard to get. Hitch,

Fender, Rushby, Reay – the canny operator juggled with his resources, every bowler was on a line and on a spot, the fielding of a celebrated fielding side excelled even its own reputation. As a close fielder on the leg side Hitch had no contemporary parallel; he was in the tradition of the great A. O. Jones, which would pass down the years with the development of leg-stump attack until it was virtually perfected in the great Surrey combination of the fifties, with Stuart Surridge and Tony Lock the immortal stars. Bill Hitch was one of those. Fender was a brilliant slip-fielder; Sandham could challenge Hendren as the fleetest-footed of the country's out-fielders; Jack Hobbs was by this time universally recognized as the greatest cover-point in the world, a lightly moving unobtrusive ranger with sure quick hands and a throw like a rifle-shot; and behind the wicket, standing up even to Hitch, little visible above his huge pads but a companionable grin, was Herbert Strudwick, one of the classic wicket-keepers of all time, radiating affability and menace. And patrolling the middle distances was the man who had come in for Donald Knight, the Oxford Blue Miles Howell, a studious and capable defensive batsman but a fieldsman fit to be mentioned along with Skeet, a glorious runner and sure catcher, a thrilling memory still. Warner even amid the tensions of this gruelling stand, noted him with an endearing touch of his own characteristic humour that so enjoyed itself that it was earnest for us all to share it – 'Howell ran so fast', he says, finding difficulty in articulating through the chuckle, 'that I christened him Spion Kop'.[1] Dear Plum!

The long stand between Warner and Hendren ground painfully on. Or perhaps 'painfully' is not quite the right word, although the systematic blocking of his scoring shots must certainly have irked Hendren; let me rather substitute 'absorb-

---

[1] Spion Kop, for the uninitiated, was the Derby winner of that year. Other similar examples of Warner's self-quoted wit are in his reminiscences. I have not found it comfortable to transcribe them; let this one serve.

ingly'. It was good hard cricket, played at a high tense level;
two good batsmen chained down by the vigour and resource
of eleven good bowlers and fielders, and 20,000 (or rather by
now nearly 30,000, and more coming in every minute)
committed enthusiasts sharing the cumulative burdens.

The luncheon interval came and went; they shut the gates
at 3.15. Latecomers were crowded twenty deep on the grass,
the playing area was closely threatened, and to ease the
pressure an hour or two later a double row was strung along
the grass in front of the sacred Pavilion itself. Without book
I cannot say whether this has ever happened before or since,
but I would guess not; and leaving out of account the Bank
Holiday crowds at the Oval in the year when Hobbs was on
the point of breaking W. G.'s record of centuries, I doubt
whether a London ground has ever harboured a crowd of these
dimensions for a match which was not a Test.

Concentrated defensive batsmanship blunted Surrey's prime
penetrative rush. They still bowled with disciplined accuracy
and fielded with menacing keenness; but Hendren and Warner
played canny and played safe, Hendren making all the
adventurous strokes on feet which were younger and springier,
Warner restricted partly by necessity and partly by tactic to
steady and solidifying techniques of obstruction. Slowly they
built 53 runs on to the meagre total that they had inherited;
88 for 3 was considerably healthier than 35 for 3; the jammed
spectators in the stands, on the benches, on the grass, willed
every run out of the batsmen with a collective fervour that
could be felt.

A superb panoramic photograph of the scene at this very
phase decorates Warner's autobiography. Shot from the old
Grand Stand, it takes in the teeming Mound, the scoreboard,
the Tavern, the dense clusters along the balconies and the
ringside. Bill Hitch on the far left is at the last phase of his
follow-through – the grunt is almost audible. Hendren the non-
striker, in no mood to run, stands placidly on his heels, while

Rushby at mid-off, black socks for the moment not in evidence, moves expectantly a pace or two forward. Neither he nor anyone else is likely to be much troubled; for Warner at the crease, back to camera, head over ball, has just executed a perfect classical forward defensive stroke, straight back down to the wicket and no complications. Jack Hobbs, limber and unmistakable at cover, is ready but will not be needed. The vigilant Strudwick, who has clearly been right up on the stumps even to an England fast bowler, is on the point of darting forward to pick up should the stroke fail to carry. Strung out illimitably behind him are a backward point (Gillie Reay, just straightened from the crouch) and four slips, Peach, Fender, Ducat and Shepherd, wonderfully poised like a *corps de ballet*. At the moment when this was taken, Sandham would have been moving in from deep third man, away out of the picture on the far right, and Miles Howell preparing to do his Spion Kop act at wide mid-on just out of the picture on the far left – or, if we must cover all contingencies, the other way round; I do not know which of them was at which end, but the whole imaginative picture is not quite complete without them and I felt bound to fill it in. The spontaneous organization of this picture is a dramatic, a kinetic triumph. Every man on the field – and there are two umpires too, each alerted, and the bowlers' umpire going on tiptoe for clearer vision – every man on the field is poised for action, integrated with the drama of which this is the happy record of a crucial phase, every figure is drawn intently as if on intricately manipulated wires towards a magnetic centre which is the nearly invisible but ever so palpable ball. It is one of the finest and most vivid cricket photographs that I have ever seen; it emphasizes not only the physical actuality, but also the dramatic idea, the symbolic crisis, of this great cricket match which was the crown and culmination of this great season; enshrines it so that we only have to look at it once and the whole essence of that fifty-year-old moment, that means so much more than a moment,

is instantly conveyed to us as freshly and as movingly as if it
had happened but a day or two ago.

For there in the very centre of it is Plum Warner, deep in
the concentration of his last and greatest battle; and for those
of us who are now living it through with him again, inch by
inch, the scoreboard tells a tale with an ominous irony unseen
behind its figures. For the total displayed on it is 88 for 3, last
man 12 (Harry Lee, remember) – last wicket fell at 35, therefore the stand now adds up to a most meritorious 53. Number
4 not out 41, Number 5 not out 18, bowlers 8 (Hitch) and 9
(Reay). Fender has gone back to pace, fast and fast-medium,
as the batsmen will not fall for his spinners; the fact that
Strudwick is right up suggests that possibly Hitch can, after
the morning's efforts, no longer be expected to go flat out – it
is possible that this is a moment where cool consolidation,
calm straight bat and cool poise, can be shown to have defeated
the first onslaught – a moment of hopeful pleasure, perhaps,
for the central figure with whom we surely cannot help
identifying. Yet the irony resides in our later knowledge that
in the next over, or at least very soon after, before any more
runs were on the board, Number 4, which was Hendren, was
bowled by Reay – dragged it on to his wicket, but bowled for
all that – for this same score of 41, and 88 for four was by no
means so happy as 88 for three, and all was in a measure to do
again.

The departure of Hendren at this stage drove Warner still
further into his shell. Dispassionate observers, now and at the
time, have been convinced that part of his trouble stemmed of
course from his side's critical position, but part from the fact
that he was badly out of form and fighting to regain it. If so
this innings was a signal triumph of character. The whole of
his account of this stage of the game contrives to insist on the
impossibility of getting the ball away. Undoubtedly Surrey
clamped tightly down on the known Middlesex aggressors;
Mann, who followed Hendren, could not open his powerful

shoulders to any effect at all, and frustration at the un-
accustomed crampings induced him to choose the wrong ball
from Fender to drive. Fender clung on to the c and b with
predatory glee; and Haig's native cheerfulness was signally
subdued. Neither of these free batsmen found insuperable
difficulty in staying in, but neither of them found any ready
opportunities to score. If the intended tactics were for Warner
to anchor himself while the two freer spirits forced the pace,
the bowlers and fielders saw to it that it did not work that way.
Tension, determination, responsibility, native character,
moulded Warner's innings that day; an unnatural uncertainty
shaped the contributions of the others. Instead of scoring while
he defended, they found themselves neck and neck with him;
when Gillie Reay brought one sharply back at Haig and
bowled him, the score since Hendren's dismissal had advanced
by 61 only, of which Mann made 12 and Haig 18. 149 for six
had the look of a parlous situation; and Warner, absently
contemplating Hobbs and Sandham as they moved and chatted
among their fellows between wickets, must have been
threatened by presages of horror and destruction before
buckling composedly to the matter in hand once more.

It was just on tea-time when Stevens came in. He has
recorded that he did not feel nervous; one of his notable
assets was an upstanding confidence in his own considerable
capacities, and this was just the confidence that this crisis
called for. He implies too that what had removed all likelihood
of nervousness was the strong reliability of the firmly-en-
trenched 'General'. 'With Plum at the other end everything
seemed well', he says, and we can sense his own feeling of
security as he came in past the thick crowds to meet the older
man's encouraging smile – 'and', he continues, 'I found
scoring at an average rate not too difficult, for the Surrey
bowling was of no great merit.' I hope he was generously
supported in his opinion of the bowling by Skeet, Lee, Hearne,
Hendren, Mann and Haig – even by his captain himself, who

had worn himself to a shadow that fine day digging precious runs out of a perfect wicket against this unmeritorious battery – but his comment is justified in the upshot, for he showed the only aggression of the innings. By this time, no doubt, the fierce keen onslaught was beginning to tire; and whatever friend or foe said of Warner's innings at the time, it had worn the penetrating edge off the bowling as nobody else had done. When Stevens arrived Warner's score was in the forties; when he left an hour and a half later, he had shown the crowded benches a range of attacking strokes that nobody, not even Hendren, had bettered, had helped his captain to add 90 most valuable runs to the rather tottery score to which he had come in, and had collected 53 of them himself in an exhilarating piece of liveliness which did everyone a power of good. Warner himself rested easy, very tired now and letting the young man have his head, happy to watch the scoreboard clicking up to the 200 and past it, giving something like respectable substance to what would otherwise have seemed a dreary and bootless labour. Stevens' breezy and optimistic innings, enlivened in its very early stages by Fender, of all people on earth, putting a dolly on the grass in the slips, the only blemish on a superb day's out-cricket, was more than a breath of air: it was as it turns out (like so many individual contributions in this match) of vital importance to the final result.

Just after six o'clock Fender broke through Stevens' defence and he played on; and almost immediately Longman was whistled away by the same bowler's imperious guile. Murrell and Warner shut up shop for the night, stubbornly fighting off the last concerted attacks of that gruelling day. The packed tired thousands roared Warner home with admiration and gratitude, recognizing, whether they put it into words or not, the knowledge, discipline, courage, and sheer character that had been forced into that exhaustive and exhausting innings. He had come in at five past one, he had come back undefeated at half past six, about four and a half hours playing time, and all he had to show for it on the board was 70 not out.

Jack Hobbs commented mildly later that he thought Warner was playing the wrong game. 'If I had been in his place, I would not have followed his tactics', said the Master, allowing perhaps of his charity too little for Warner's age, responsibility, comparative physical frailty, and undisputed technical inferiority to himself. Hobbs spoke more in admiring sympathy than in censure, and went on to acknowledge that as things turned out Warner had been right (there is however no reason to suppose that if he had scored 50 more runs things would not have turned out even better than they did). However, Hobbs was not the only one to express disappointment with the Middlesex score. They had been in all day and made 253 for 8, and a number of Middlesex supporters in a state of disgruntlement dismissed their county's Championship chances for ever and a day and were inclined to throw the blame on Warner's funereal progress. Stevens' later comment that without the captain's innings the whole performance would have been a complete catastrophe and Murrell's immediate spoken one that 250 runs took a lot of making can perhaps be regarded as putting the whole question, if question there be, into a more reasonable perspective.

Any weekend qualms suffered by Middlesex well-wishers can hardly have been allayed by the news from Lancashire; a heavy dew had affected the Old Trafford wicket, Lancashire had exultantly put Worcestershire in, and bundled them out for 124 with easy self-confidence; they had then got to 114 for three at the close of play, and gave every indication of having the match comfortably in the bag. Lancashire supporters, reading the Middlesex score and knowing even better than anyone in London that a Middlesex defeat or draw would give Lancashire the Championship provided they made no mistake over Worcestershire, consumed their cowheel and pigs' trotters with a genial contentment.

Warner put his fears and doubts in his pocket; the match was still wide open as far as he was concerned, and there was little point in counting chickens, live or dead. He began again on Monday where he had left off on Saturday, hopeful as ever; the day, he says, was fine, which means it did not rain; but the keen recollection of Mr. Alec Waugh, whose memories of this match as published in *The Cricketer* so valuably reinforce those of Warner and Stevens, establishes it as a grey enough morning. The sun that had shone on Saturday did not appear, and the Middlesex innings did not go on for very long either. Warner got to 79 before Rushby beat and bowled him; and in the next over Murrell touched Bill Hitch into the slips and all was over. 268 was the score, and nobody will say that this was negligible; but I doubt if anyone with the interests of Middlesex at heart felt particularly sanguine about it.

Less so, I imagine, when Hobbs and Sandham began to play the opening bowlers with all the time in the world. There is no need at this stage to dilate upon the easy mastery of Jack Hobbs; in 1920 he was in the fullest possible flow, was heading for his highest seasonal aggregate yet (which he beat later, but that is another story), and was in that kind of confident form in which he knew himself to be capable of reducing to instant ribbons any bowling offered to him from anyone in the universe. Compact and watchful at the other end, his partner was about to develop into as formidable a combination of impregnability and grace as any batsman I can name; shortish, light and quick on his small feet, elegant of body and wrist movement, Andrew Sandham built up over the years a wonderful consistency. We see him here in the earlier stages of a career in which he attained an individual greatness which, because it was shadowed by the close proximity of genius, never had its due recognition. This appeared to disturb him very little; he was at all times supremely efficient in the role for which his fate and his talent had cast him.

Hobbs and Sandham saw off Durston and Haig without

trouble, picking up their runs in the way they were to exploit so well down the decade – easy placed single here, delicate deflection there, inexcusably short run judged to a nicety, two sudden cracking fours – the pattern built itself up, there was speed but no hurry. The figures spun on the scoreboard, 30 up, 40 up, 50 up, unresting, there was nothing like the buffeting uphill struggle of Saturday, it was as if a finely-tuned engine ran with no noise or vibration. It all looked so easy that maybe Hobbs for once treated it as if it really were so. The spinners had come on, the two were coolly taking their measure, necessary adjustments in technique were being made – when Hobbs let out at a well-pitched-up ball from Hearne which hung a little, or which through casualness he mistimed a trifle. He meant it to go past mid-off for four, and it would have done, it was O.K. for speed; but it lifted and it went straight as a bullet to mid-off, and Frank Mann never put chances like that on the floor. 24 was all very well in its way, but it wasn't what they had been fearing from Hobbs; and the roar that ran round the crowded ground was a testimony to the sudden explosion of liberating relief.

Sandham impassively took over. It was to be one of his great days, and he went into it with his usual methodical coolness. The score sheet shows what looks very like a nasty little collapse after Hobbs' dismissal, but the fact that none of the chroniclers mentions it, and that all of them record an impression of a capable quick-scoring Surrey overhauling their opponents with ready ease, seems to redound almost entirely to Sandham's personal credit. Whatever was happening at one end, and many and various things clearly went on there, there was constant unwinking mastery at the other. Warner soon brought Durston back and kept him manfully at it, ringing the alternative changes principally on Hearne, Lee and Stevens; runs came fairly freely off all of them, mainly through Sandham, who was at home with each and every one and was not particular off whom he scored. Had Joe Murrell been a thought quicker in reaction, he could have stumped him when he had made 40, and a slip catch went to grass at 77; otherwise his display was without flaw, and he covered with unpretentious competence the shortcomings of the others.

Miles Howell, Spion Kop in the field, did not exploit much speed when he batted. He never did, he was stolid and un-adventurous, though his batting had an admirable and cour-ageous solidity. This time he left the second-wicket scoring to Sandham and was caught at the wicket sparring at Durston; and his immediate successor, Tom Shepherd, a red-faced broad-shouldered aggressor a little new to the business as yet but destined to be a familiar delight at the Oval for a dozen years to come, went the same way home in the next over without scoring. But Warner failed to get his breakthrough; the next batsman was the cheerful Alan Peach, whose most recent innings had been 200, a chubby bandy-legged individual of great optimism who was later to be used primarily as a stock bowler but who in this year of 1920 was being regarded almost exclusively as an attacking early batsman. He had great blacksmith's forearms and a hawk's eye, and developed as the years went on into one of the most entertaining of random bashers that the Oval has ever harboured; at the present stage he was neither one thing nor the other, perhaps, like the man in *Love's Labour's Lost*, 'an excellent good neighbour i' faith and a very good bowler; but as Alexander, alas, a little o'erparted'. Yet he stayed and made 18 sensibly and valuably, while Sandham tried out at the other end his capacious repertory of beguiling strokes. Stevens at last, whom Sandham was playing and punishing without worry, forced Peach back on to his wicket and induced him to hit it; an encouraging moment, but at this particular phase a moment only, since the next batsman to arrive, Andy Ducat, was perhaps at this exact stage in cricket history the third best batsman on that very strong batting list and was coming in deceptively low in the order.

Ducat was a beautifully-built, athletic player, a handsome and forward-playing stylist. In the glorious roll-call of Surrey's classic batting in the twenties he was to be the utterly reliable Number Three. On this day of Surrey's momentarily faltering progress he batted with a square positive resolution that destroyed all Middlesex hopes that their opponents were going to waver. Fender may or may not have dictated his tactics but whatever was behind it he chose at once to attack. This not only set the score going at a useful pace again, but it gave Sandham a very valuable space to breathe. His adventurous habits led him to take risks that Sandham was too wily to indulge in, and his equable temper enabled him to remain unperturbed when Hearne or Stevens beat him. He was that kind of batsman to whom fast bowling appealed considerably more readily than slow, and he faced Durston with something like relish. Pacing Sandham run for run, he stepped up the scoring rate to a run and a half a minute; and as the culmination of the most exhilarating partnership, so far, in the whole match, he cracked Durston for four fours in one over and brought the stand's tally to ninety runs in just under the hour. The full hundred partnership was achieved, all but a single run, before he ventured out injudiciously to Lee and was neatly stumped: 49 to Ducat, 99 to the partnership, and I doubt if even a rabid Middlesex partisan would have grudged the extra run, whatever delight there may have been at the sight of his receding back.

Percy Fender's rangy and high-spirited batsmanship was in its very element here. His beaky menacing figure stalked in upon a situation where high adventurous competence had laid the game at his feet. All the Surrey innings wanted now was a hitter to come in and hit, to bang home the skilfully-contrived advantage and bang it home conclusively. Percy Fender spat on his hands and banged. Neither Hearne nor Stevens were at their best and he treated them as he pleased; and in his present mood, fortified as it was by his pleasurable extravagances at

Northampton, he was ready and willing to take on anybody
Middlesex could offer him whether they happened to be bowling at their best or not. Durston, in fact, was bowling with
remarkable steadiness; it did not stop Fender punching as
many holes in him as in his colleagues. Once again Sandham,
now up above the hundred mark and as demurely contained
as always, was able to take his ease, as the score imperceptibly
bounded.

Fender's innings lasted no time at all; he rattled up 30 in
what Warner calls 'a very few minutes'; he gave a catch to
Haig off Durston and departed satisfied enough, though I do
not doubt that he would have liked twenty or thirty more, if
it could have been managed in the time. Hitch and Reay,
timed to follow him in and carry on his work, were ready
enough to try; and Fender no doubt worried less at his own
dismissal than he would have done if he had had fewer batsmen
in reserve whom he knew to be as glad to cut loose as he. As
it happened, neither Hitch nor Reay did a thing, and all that
they, or Strudwick and Rushby in their turn after them,
could do was to hold the other end up successively while
Sandham took final charge, enlivening the latter end of this
prolific innings, the Middlesex first innings total having been
duly waved to in passing, by showing the whole range of his
strokes all over again in sequence, specializing in the square
and late cut but never stinting himself on the rest. With the
last pair in and the runs still clicking up smoothly, Fender
declared with a lead of 73, wisely and malevolently giving the
tired Middlesex batsmen a nasty three-quarters of an hour in
the uniform evening greyness. The vast packed crowd (if not
as many as Saturday's, yet only a very few hundreds short of
it), recognized and could not help approving the rational good
sense of the tactics; a couple of good wickets down that same
night in the gloaming, an early couple in the morning while
the dew was still on the grass, and where could Middlesex
be? Somewhere not yet near level, with four men out; who

would give a thank you for their last Championship chances now?

Fender, coming lightly down the Pavilion steps with Reay and Howell to meet Jack Hobbs and the clustered professionals for their spirited evening assault on the weary Middlesex opening batsmen, must have stepped out to the middle with as cheerful and hopeful an air as any captain could possibly expect to affect at this stage of a well-fought game. The honours and the likelihoods were clearly on Surrey's side; the day so far had belonged without dispute first to Sandham, undefeated with 167 after as comely and courageous a show of major batting skills as anyone but Hobbs on the two sides could command, and second to Surrey itself, who had been manoeuvred by skill and good luck into a position of wonderful advantage, which a couple or so of decisive blows delivered briskly and sharply that night would make virtually unassailable. Nevertheless, the spice in the situation was that the certainty still had to be made good. The batsmen now preparing to bat out the evening were not on an entirely perfunctory mission; it was up to the fielding side to destroy the equilibrium, but the equilibrium did still, quite palpably, exist. Middlesex supporters, however gloomily convinced of the fatal probabilities, retained sufficient generosity to roar Sandham home in admiration of one of the greatest innings seen at Lord's in even that season of great innings, and sufficient breath and zest to settle themselves for the ordeal of living through the last agonizing minutes during which Hitch and Rushby, now happily flexing their rested muscles, would throw everything they had and more also at the Middlesex defenders.

Skeet and Lee, resting their feet as best they might while resignedly buckling on their pads, needed no instructions or encouragement even from their most authoritative and sympathetic leader. What he said to them I do not know; no doubt his instinctive tact induced him to say as little as possible.

They tracked out in the grey evening to the welcoming applause with but little in their heads but the hope and intention to be there and undisturbed when the merciful clock-hands dismissed them for the night.

Bill Hitch opened up from the Nursery End with his wide umbrella of four slips and barely two or three men in front of the wicket, coming in for the kill as if the devil were at his back. Tom Rushby, less spectacular but a thought more naggingly accurate, flashed his black socks from the Pavilion End, encouraging no freedom of stroke. Skeet and Lee, both small men, shrank compactly into hard emblems of defiance – Skeet swarthy, dark-eyed, broody, Lee snub-nosed and pugnacious, an unperturbed old sweat giving a damn for no bowler alive. Anything on the wicket got the full face of the bat; anything off the wicket got a dirty look, nothing more. The slips bent and unbent to no avail, Strudwick alone got exercise chucking the ball back. Middlesex supporters and players, agonizing their way through this last dreadful half hour, felt a trifle less uneasy when Lee was the striker; Skeet's determination was never in question, only his experience and skill. Lee was a seasoned warrior with over 1,200 runs in his personal bag already this year; Skeet had spent half the summer batting number nine at Oxford, Lee had spent half his life doing just what he was doing now, seeing the shine off and making life easy for others. They watched Lee with approval, they prayed for Skeet with fervour. The concentrated intensity of the communal goodwill helped to key him up to a new authority and reliability. With every over completed, his confidence grew; and so, correspondingly, did Lee's, and the crowd's, and Warner's.

It must have been irking to Fender. He had bought by his own aggressiveness and his team's response to it this precious three-quarters of an hour in which Middlesex were to be as vulnerable as they ever would, when his bowlers would be fresh and the batsmen tired and apprehensive, when a quick

blow or two would have capsized the opposition beyond
recovery. And now his bowlers had fierily and enthusiastically
delivered their destroying blow – and nothing had happened.
The batsmen still looked suspiciously down the wicket, left
the rising balls alone, put broad bats to the inswingers, tickled
the odd run here and there; but the shine was going off the
ball, there was less apprehensiveness in their defensive position-
ing, there was even a confident attacking stroke or two. He
tried a bowling change; it did not work. Skeet and Lee, their
jaws set, came to six-thirty with a relief that was shared by
every well-wisher on the ground; they had got to 27 un-
scathed and that was enough for to-night. Tomorrow was
another day. I imagine that they slept sound.

Whether Warner did so or not has never been stated. The
news from Old Trafford, whether in the old way of these
things he heard it late on the Monday night or whether he had
to wait until Tuesday morning's paper for it, was in no way
encouraging. Lancashire, having been set 99 to win, were
comfortably halted at 59 for no wicket, and short of a down-
pour the northern county seemed to be home and dry. There
was therefore nothing for it but to win this Surrey match;
and Skeet and Lee, putting their pads on again, knew it in
their bones that they must get ahead very quickly indeed.

The atmosphere in the Middlesex camp was one of resolution
rather than optimism. Stevens remembers that feelings were
mixed. 'We all felt we had a good chance and no more', he
says, adding that they were dead keen to do it for 'the General'
and, or should it be *but*, leaned heavily on him. Warner
himself records a general opinion that Middlesex could not win,
but never suggests that he shared it. Letters, telegrams, bunches
of white heather, a heartening paraphernalia of goodwill,
crowded the dressing-room. The Tuesday crowd was, not
unnaturally, smaller than those of the other two days, but
12,000 paid, which was a phenomenon altogether out of the
ordinary then and would need new words to be coined to

describe it now. Surrey agreeably hopeful, Middlesex more dubiously so, the match resumed.

Skeet and Lee were visited with just one adventitious piece of luck that somehow has never got lifted out of the newspapers into the histories. When the Surrey team took the field Hitch was missing. He had apparently had trouble with a strained foot, the discomfort had reasserted itself overnight, and he was still having treatment for it when play started. Rushby and Reay were hostile and accurate enough with the still shining ball, but in the bright fresh morning air the extra yard or two of pace that the fast bowler could generate might have afforded Skeet and Lee just that little more unsettling discomfort at the beginning. He was only off the field for an hour; but by the time he came back into the attack their confidence was double what it had been at the start.

Skeet and Lee appear to have gone about the uphill business with quite unusual promptitude. What surprises me as I read the standard accounts of this stage of the game is the perfunctory way in which it gets passed over, as if it was all in the day's work. The county started off on this fearful haul 46 runs behind, two batsmen not only to dig in but pile on extremely rapid runs, turning a probable defeat into what may be tremblingly hailed as potential victory, and nobody gives us anything but the bare facts. I don't say that they withhold praise – there is plenty of generous recognition – but the *facts* are presented as if they are accountable. Which they barely are. Two batsmen, one very skilled but not unusually adventurous or quick-scoring, the other a near novice despite immense character and courage, weather a most unpleasant overnight assault and return to their task on a very crucial day to such effect that in two hours – two early hours on a Lord's wicket in late August, dew on the grass and all that that entails – in *two hours* they add 172. Two batsmen of no conspicuous reputation for brilliance score with apparent ease at 86 runs an hour, and nobody is surprised at this. Warner simply says that 'they obtained an early supremacy over the Surrey bowling'. Stevens says they put on 208 for the first wicket. You bet your sweet life they did both of these things. But nobody has described how or why it can have happened like this; and so inexorably quickly, too. Fifty years later, the enquiring heart of a Surrey man is shaken not only with regret, and with admiration, but with wonder. If it had been Hendren and Mann there would be no surprise; but it wasn't, it was Skeet and Lee. It may be, of course, that in those dear dead days beyond recall 86 an hour was considered nothing out of the ordinary; I am confirmed in this conjecture by a comment in one of the contemporary newspapers about Stevens' stand with Warner on the Saturday night. 'Together', says this organ of contemporary opinion, 'they added 90 runs in an hour; it was not a brisk rate of progress.' I can only hope, for his sake, that the gentleman who wrote this is not alive to consider whether his words would apply to-day.

Skeet and Lee took the Surrey bowling and played with it as they pleased; the lift of heart that their superb enterprise must have given to Warner and their fellows must have been indescribably elating. Fender switched his bowlers without cease, but got no present comfort. I think it quite likely that some of the bewildering secret must reside in the fact that these same bowlers had bowled themselves out on Saturday and, however the accounts praise their steadiness, were below their best. Hitch was away for a vital hour; when he came back he could engender no venom whatever. Rushby and Reay tried hard, Fender improvised all he could. Lee took charge, going over from his so familiar technique of patient but productive defence to a newly-commanded regime of disciplined and ruthless attack. Particularly he risked lbw many times by hooking with power and effectiveness off the middle stump; he went out of his common way to force opportunities to make runs. When the hundred went up his score was 62; after this, Skeet began to do a little on his own account, using

the cut in preference to other strokes, gaining confidence with
every run scored. In the second half of this extraordinary pre-
lunch period, Skeet was pacing Lee almost neck and neck.

Who will dare to say whose efforts won this match? –
everyone in Middlesex did something to win it, whether the
score-sheet proclaims it or not. But psychologically at any rate,
Skeet and Lee won it on this Tuesday morning. Surrey walked
out on to the field at 11.30 in high-spirited confidence; they
trailed in at lunch-time in what must have been at the very
least, angry frustration, and at the worst, resigned despondency.
Two batsmen not of the very first rank had taken their attack
and made a joke of it, and what is more taken the initiative
clean away from the attackers. Middlesex would probably
now be able not so much to force a win as to jockey herself
into a position from which it would be thinkable to force one.
This was not the same as being assured of victory, not by half;
but it looked by now just possible that they would not be
easily defeated, and this was the first time in the match that
anybody with the interests of Middlesex at heart could
seriously think of it in those terms.

Lee got to his great hundred a few moments before lunch.
In his long career he made 37 of these hundreds – none of them
could have been of this masterly and significant quality; for
in making it he had uplifted not only himself but his partner
to uncommon heights of skill, and injected a new quality
into this most crucial of all the matches he ever played in. He
went in to the enormous applause, 102 not out, Middlesex 199
for no wicket, knowing that his side were now 126 runs on
and that he and his partner had provided out of nothing but
their own sturdy resolution an unexpected springboard for
victory. Skeet with his highly meritorious 88 not out must
have felt happy and fulfilled too, Warner's radiant reception
of him being but the joyful crown of a morning in which all
imagined terrors had been faced and overcome.

(A pleasant and ironic little festivity was at this moment

being conducted at Old Trafford. Lancashire had duly vanquished the unhappy Worcestershire without any difficulty whatever, and, reading nothing into the overnight scores from Lord's to lead their hard-headed practical north-country brains to suppose that Middlesex had a hope in hell of winning, had awarded themselves the Championship and begun convivially upon the champagne. Having momentarily lifted the curtain upon their celebration, let us leave them to enjoy it.)

Lancashire supporters may have spent their lunch-time golloping champagne; Middlesex followers spent theirs doing arithmetic. Alec Waugh remembers these feverish calculations vividly – they all knew that the game was going on until seven o'clock and that Surrey were one of the quickest-scoring sides in the competition. They worked it out, and neither then or at this distance of time can they be faulted – that Middlesex to get in with a chance of winning would have to set Surrey over 200 to be gone for at a speed of 80 an hour. This difficult but crucial equipoise could be achieved all right if Middlesex, now as near as made no odds 200, could contrive to add at least another 100 in about an hour and twenty minutes. Waugh implies that the supporters felt some doubt about this. I, with hindsight, and with what seems to me by now to be a fairly intimate knowledge of all the Middlesex batsmen's capacities, wonder what their worry was. 100 in eighty minutes, from Hendren, Mann, Haig, Stevens, even Jack Hearne at a pinch, seems to me a cake-walk. Lee and Skeet had managed it all right before lunch; why should the others not manage it as well after, against bowlers who had lost their spirited optimism? Come to that, neither Lee nor Skeet was out yet; there seems no reason why they could not have been expected to do the whole thing on their own while they were about it.

The odd thing was that after all they didn't make a very good fist of it. The 200 went up at once, Lee added a few singles to his pre-lunch score, the total reaching 208, Skeet was still some way away from his own hundred, when to everyone's surprise Hitch broke through Lee's defences and bowled him. Let the crowd's applause stand for the moment for all the praise due to Harry Lee for this incomparable innings; no words of mine can add to the honours – all that is relevant is implied in the achievement, a wonderful personal end to a wonderful personal season.

Warner says that he altered his batting order, calling up his quicker scorers, anxious, like Mr. Waugh and his friends around the boundary, for quick and ready runs, the quicker and readier the better. Yet contemporary newspapers indicate clearly enough that Jack Hearne went in Number Three – otherwise all that Warner did with his first innings order was to drop himself down and pull Murrell up. Hearne began in fact to score at his pacier higher rate, the one he customarily avoided for safety's sake but would only too willingly and loyally embrace if his captain or the situation demanded. He saw Skeet to his hundred – and everything that has been said of Lee should be said of Skeet too, save that his, being the innings of a far less experienced player with far fewer resources, deserves an even longer and more heartfelt round of generous acclamation. It was without doubt his finest hour. He played very little first-class cricket after this season, as his vocation took him to a lifetime's service in the Sudan; he never equalled this great feat and I doubt if he expected to. He can, and I very much hope does still, treasure this day in his memory as the greatest of his cricketing career. An awful lot of people, Surrey and Middlesex supporters alike, have never forgotten him and never will. Coming to his triumphant hundred he bought cricket immortality along with it; and a few minutes later, his work done, he touched a ball from Hitch to Fender in the slips.

It was now up to the quick scorers; and it is noticeable that they made rather less than a satisfactory job of it. Their ragged performance had its origins in the high tension that must now have been quite palpably generating in their camp; in the urgency impressed upon them by Warner; in the sense that in a curious kind of way time was against them. Batsman after batsman started hitting too soon, denied themselves even an over to get a sight of the ball. Surrey's bowling, elated by a couple of quick wickets, tightened correspondingly; a different kind of contest was suddenly on, and this time it was Middlesex, striving hard to dictate time and terms, who found themselves at a disadvantage. Hendren hit far too soon and skied the ball to deep mid-on; Hearne, who had been at a busy little deflective game of his own and proved in the end to be a more prolific contributor than the celebrated aggressors who tried to clear the fence, was leg before to Rushby trying to turn a straight ball round the corner; and although Mann enjoyed a big hit or two there was little authority or stability about his batting and he soon lost Haig, who was clean bowled for one by Rushby, whose pertinacity was at long last getting a measurable reward.

Perhaps predictably, it was Stevens who brought a little stability into the slightly feverish atmosphere. His first innings had been an admirable blend of defence and attack; and he buckled to his second in similar strain. He had injected liveliness into the first innings; he injected a kind of strengthening reassurance into this. He helped Mann raise the score to 290, when the latter skied a catch into the covers and departed; and saw the promoted Murrell instantly despatched by Reay one run later. Middlesex had lost seven wickets in an hour while 83 runs were being added – by to-day's standards almost a crash rate of scoring, in those times apparently a commonplace – and Warner clearly felt that to leave Surrey only 220 runs to get in three and a half hours or so – not much more than a run a minute required – was equivalent to offering their doughty opponents the whole of the last two days' hard labour on a silver salver. He accordingly came in at last, himself.

It was at this point that the crowd, recognizing that this was in fact a significant moment, a man coming in for the very last time to a Championship innings for the county he had virtually made his own, gave him all the welcome, the encouragement, the thanks, the goodwill and the affection that they had kept pent up in themselves for the last three days, perhaps for the season. As soon as the Harlequin cap appeared at the top of the Pavilion steps they rose to their feet as a man and roared him to the very threshold of the wicket. The applause echoed round the ground in waves as he took his solitary way, continued unabated till he stood to take guard. Dimly he perceived that the Surrey team were joining in too – the redoubled sallies of well-wishing, with this additional little generosity added, filled his eyes with tears. Then Reay ran up to bowl again, and the mist cleared, the battle was on; 'the General' was in charge again.

The short breakneck partnership which he then enjoyed with Stevens was one of the strangest and most surprising of the match. In the next seven and a half minutes these two, running for everything, added no less than 25 runs – one of the most extraordinary and successful exploitations of tip-and-run ever seen on a first-class ground. Stevens of course was nineteen, and could run for anything, and did; but Warner was forty-seven and of a frailer habit; he might have been excused for getting out of breath. But no, the stepping-up of speed came at his instigation. 'Run everything', he said to Stevens. 'I want a few runs fast.' They ran everything, and they added the runs he needed, they turned impossibilities into possibilities, ones into twos, twos into threes. They even took risks with Hobbs at cover, and got away with it, breathless, triumphant, ready for more next ball. It probably mildly demoralized the fielders. It couldn't have gone on for long without disaster, but it did not need to. Plum Warner, reverting in the very last innings of his Championship career to an irrepressible youthfulness, signed himself off with a brilliant appropriateness. He

tells of his pride at being in with young Stevens at the finish,
'he the rising star, and I whose sun was fast setting'. This we
can understand and take pleasure in on our own account;
but it is clear that in essence this partnership that lasted so little
time and yet was of so incalculable a value was not between an
old man and a young one, but between two boys together.

At any rate, the declaration came at 3.40 precisely; and
Surrey were given in effect three hours to get 244. To-day, I
feel, they would normally expire at the very idea; in 1920 the
task was seen by most spectators as carrying a fifty-fifty
chance. With Hobbs around anything might happen; and he
was by no means the only forcing batsman that had to be got
rid of. All the pros and all the cons were repetitively and
exhaustingly canvassed by everyone on the ground; and as
nothing would matter except what actually happened, everyone was secretly relieved when the bell clanged and the
umpires came out, and, for the last time in a county match,
Plum Warner led Middlesex into the field. Following them,
stepping lightly, ready, experienced, infinitely accomplished,
came Hobbs and Sandham.

Durston led off from the Nursery End at four o'clock;
Haig bowled with the Pavilion at his back. The batsmen began
as in the first innings, methodical and unhurried, knowing that
runs would come in time, meanwhile taking singles. In an
over or two the bowlers changed ends. Ten went up, then
twenty; neither batsman had as yet declared any commanding
or aggressive intention, but it would soon happen if the
innings were to get under way.

All of a sudden Haig pitched one on a perfect length on the
off stump; as Hobbs moved in to play it it went sharply away
down the hill. The snick carried hard to Hendren in the slips;
for one sickening split second he fumbled and it spun away,
Stevens in the gully had a perfect view. Lee at second slip –
it was his day all right – moved promptly in to the rescue,
snatched it inches from the ground, threw it up – and the whole

of Lord's exploded in a delighted roar. It is strange that
Warner never recorded his exact thoughts at this apocalyptic
moment, as Jack Hobbs turned from the wicket and Surrey's
hopes were halved, and Middlesex's correspondingly delight-
edly inflated, on the instant. I am a Surrey man, and my
spirits perceptibly sink, to this very day, describing it.

Miles Howell faced up to the situation admirably. His first
innings reticence was gone, and he began at once playing
freely and cheerfully, unsuspected strokes flowing out all
round the wicket. Sandham as on the day before betrayed not
an eyelid's flicker, scoring with his unobtrusive fluency at the
slightest opportunity. The two of them ran between the
wickets with promptitude and imagination; the scoreboard
was kept gently but inexorably busy. Hobbs had gone at 22,
and soon the thirties were passed and the forties; Warner tried
two bowling changes – Hearne was on at the Pavilion end,
Stevens at the other. 50 went up, and 60; the batsmen were
settling in. There was no doubt whatever about Sandham's
mastery, which he seemed to have carried over unconcernedly
from the first innings, but Howell's easy and stylish competence was a growing menace, and Surrey accomplished a
quarter of their task with an ominous smoothness. Then at 62
Stevens flighted one a shade higher, drew Howell speculatively
down the wicket and spun it sufficiently to beat the bat. Joe
Murrell had the bails off in a blink, and Middlesex exhaled a
relieved breath at the respite. Howell departed with 25 out of
40 scored for the second wicket, a valiant and useful innings.
Tom Shepherd replaced him.

Frequenters of the Oval in the twenties all remember this
sturdy equable character with affection. It is difficult to think
of him as he was in this match, slim and untried and wearing
as yet the Surrey Second Eleven cap. He may well have been
nervous, for he was playing for the place which he ultimately
occupied so reliably and prolifically, and he had made 0 in the
first innings. But he faced Stevens with a broad and deter-

mined bat, and he and Sandham began the really serious task
of matching the run-rate with the needs of the hour.

There seems little reason to suppose that the two batsmen
felt hurried; they were trained and orthodox professional
performers and they timed their scoring with some considerable skill. Warner did all he could to contain them, particularly
Sandham, who was playing even better than he had in the
first innings. The wicket was lasting beautifully – too beautifully for the spinners – and batsmen with aggressive intent had
merely to use their feet and runs could be found, if not at will,
at least at some kind of leisure. Shepherd began to try out some
of the handsome drives which so dignified the Oval in later
seasons. The two of them had the hundred up when the
innings had been going for seventy-five minutes. 244 to win,
and 100 for 2 accomplished; Surrey supporters felt a pleasurable
mixture of excitement and content. The failure of Hobbs had
begun to lose its tragic implications.

Percy Fender, something restless on the balcony, was not
entirely satisfied. Realizing, I suppose, that however level
Surrey were keeping now there was bound to be a slump in
the scoring rate should a wicket or wickets fall, he felt strongly
that the more runs could be got into the immediate bag the
better, and who more equipped to do this than two forcing
batsmen of quality well set? So he made a sign for them to
step it up a bit.

Plum Warner saw that sign and drew his own conclusions.
During the last quarter of an hour or so of the Sandham-
Shepherd stand, Stevens had been rested; but he brought him
back again now, at the Nursery end, and he dropped Hendren
back from short leg into the outfield – a manoeuvre simple
and logical enough in the re-telling of it, but with a touch of
neat brilliance in its logic and simplicity. The bowlers went on
bowling, and the batsmen went on batting. 110 went up, and
120 – Surrey were virtually half-way to victory, precisely half
the allotted time had gone, two accomplished batsmen were

cruising well within themselves, there was no venom in the wicket and (to speak frankly) not much in the bowling. Surrey, after a somewhat frustrating morning and afternoon, were on the point of riding home, on the high waves, in the golden evening.

At this happy point Shepherd let out with all the power of his shoulders at a half-volley from Stevens. Or perhaps I do the bowler an injustice – it may be that Shepherd thought it was a half-volley and behaved accordingly, and that the bowler had cunningly dropped it a few inches shorter. At any rate the full-blooded straight drive soared as high as heaven towards the Nursery end boundary; and Hendren, losing the flight at first against the crowded Pavilion, deftly adjusted his position, backed and backed until he was almost up against the sight screen, and took a superb catch high up by his right shoulder only a yard or two inside the line. The enormous roar for this memorable feat merged into the generous and merited applause for the retiring batsman; it signalled, without any of the vociferous spectators or animated players knowing any-thing about it, the decisive turning point of this astonishing game.

This was of course not at all clear yet; and the appearance of Fender, promoting himself two places up the order, made it quite clear that he and his county were going to meet the situation with an appropriate belligerence. The Surrey section of the crowd greeted his arrival with a great storm of cheering, and from the very first he proclaimed his intention to satisfy them. The batsmen had crossed while Shepherd's drive hung in the air above Hendren; Sandham tickled a single at once, and Fender immediately put his whole ferocious weight and power into a square slash off Stevens that Warner got his right hand to with some courage, preventing a certain four but not the snatched single. There seems some indication that Fender was a trifle over-anxious – at any rate whether through over-anxiety or through a natural inability to stop a lightning yorker on the leg stump, he was clean bowled by Durston in the next over and Surrey were 122 for four.

You can almost sense the sudden elation that must have risen in the Middlesex eleven like a tide. Two quick wickets of this kind – one menacing well-set batsman, one even more menacing batsman cut off at once – always play havoc with the smoothly-generated pace of an innings, and in this particular instance sadly unbalanced it. The fielders chattered excitedly, they could feel a new heady resolution forming. Alan Peach, the new batsman, arrived under a disadvantage; instead of coming in to polish the match off with a few genial blows, he had to build a substantial innings in support of the perennial Sandham, and see to it that the sudden set-backs did not cause vital delay. He began manfully – he was a brisk batsman who could hit, when he liked, quite murderously; and although he was hardly an equal substitute for Fender, he was of Fender's mind and temper. He buckled down to it at once; he had a crisp, wristy, aggressive style, and he made the fielders wring their hands if they put them in the way.

Durston having temporarily done what was required, Hearne took over again at the Pavilion end. Stevens from the Nursery end bothered Peach with the variety of his flight – Sandham, with ample reserves of time to play his shots, took less account of bowlers, concentrating his mind on scoring opportunities. Peach made a few hard hits, Sandham persuasively inserted his quota of runs from delicate insinuations and deflections, yet he scored as fast as Peach. By just about a quarter to six they had got the score to 143, 101 to win in 75 minutes, by no means impossible given health and strength but a tough task none the less – when Peach faltered forward at Stevens and was lost when a beautifully spun leg-break pitched on a perfect length on the leg stump and hit the top of the off. Middlesex were tightening the pressure, but Andy Ducat, they did well to remember, was a mighty good bat to be going in Number Seven, Sandham was apparently indestructible, and Hitch at least could hit like the devil when roused, as well he might be to-day.

Ducat showed as always the broadest possible face of the bat. There was absolutely no reason why he and Sandham, given a few minutes of reasonable settling in, should not step up the scoring and make good the victory after all. And there never is, in these cases, any reason why the possibility should not be rendered down into fact. Except of course that there are always at least two possibilities; and one may be forgiven, after a lifetime of following this prodigiously complex game with an essentially simple mind, for suggesting that it is the other possibility that always seems to come true. Sandham and Ducat were on a loser, and in their hearts they probably knew it, but being tough fighters would not acknowledge it. And we must not leave out of account the entirely praiseworthy fact that Sandham until this precise moment of time had been on the field throughout the entire gruelling match. He had every excuse for being bone-weary; but he continued to put confident bat to ball with his unremitting watchfulness and circumspection until four minutes to six, when to the huge surprise of everybody on the ground, and by now this totted up to 20,000 or so, he hit a full-pitch back to Hearne and was caught and bowled. He had made in a bare two hours 68 runs of immense character and value to add on to his monumental not out hundred of the first innings. Middlesex, cheering him relievedly all the way home, must have felt that they were losing an old and valued friend. The shrewder Surrey supporters present, looking at the time and what was left of the batting, began seriously to write this match off.

It must have been about now that Warner's composure, preserved superbly not only through this match but through the fierce gauntlet-run of all the other matches here chronicled, began to be invaded by tensions and excitements. Until Shepherd got out he can barely have dared to hope; for the last half-hour while Sandham held up Surrey's equilibrium, his native caution enjoined an unambitious neutrality of expectation – he hardly dared look at the prospect. Now, with Sandham gone, the Championship actuality must have opened up thunderously before him. No wonder he felt, for the first time, rattled and excited. Here was the end, now all but within reach of his outstretched hand, towards which he and his team had so consistently, untiringly, excitedly, lovingly battled. And here he was with them on the field, in a Championship fixture, for the very last time, for the very last few minutes of the very last time. Stevens or Hearne bowling, Murrell bending behind the stumps, Lee and Haig crouching in the slips, Hendren prowling anywhere, Mann at mid-off, Skeet in the deep – they had lately become strangely cherished extensions of himself, part of his sleeping and waking, dear and inseparable companions who relied upon him and upon whom he relied. He would see and know them all again, but never like this; they were friends and helpers who, he suddenly realized, were bringing him, and bringing him in a very few minutes now, to the greatest and happiest public triumph of his career, to an end which only a short time ago he would never have dreamed would be possible. And it wouldn't have been possible without them; nor, as they would severally insist later, would it have been possible without him. Together they had been able to perfect the techniques necessary to succeed in this exhilarating and triumphant corporate enterprise; time and time again they had rejoiced together in hard-won success, and it now looked as they would at last and against odds achieve the culminating reward. And it would still be the very last time that he would play together with them like this. The joy that would be almost too sweet to be borne would be balanced by a regret that nothing could properly allay. No wonder that Warner, fielding through the last few overs of this astonishing match, was prey to conflicting emotions to which he could never give adequate expression.

He was sharply distracted from any tendency to self-pity when Bill Hitch hit his first ball hard to deep square leg and Patsy Hendren, enjoying a rather mixed afternoon as far as catching was concerned, put a knee-high chance on the carpet to the sound of not unreasonable local disappointment. Alec Waugh records that this fearful blow to his hopes convinced him that Hitch would now proceed to win the match off his own bat, but he was soon to know, and the world very soon after, that it is not often that summary justice of this kind is done, and it certainly wasn't done then. Hitch tried a hit or two, but there was instability in the air; it spread first to Ducat, Surrey's last batting hope, who misjudged Hearne's googly in the next over and was out leg before. And only a few balls later, Stevens, now bowling as well as ever he had performed during the season, clean bowled Hitch with a googly of his own, eight wickets were down for 168, there were still fifty minutes to play, and all the life had drained out of the Surrey resistance.

The last two wickets were not to fall immediately; in Warner's heightened state of tensed and tingling awareness (and, no doubt, when I say Warner's, I should add the rest of his team too) the minutes probably seemed like hours. But anyone with half an eye could have realized that the rot had got well into Surrey and that it was only a question of time – not really very much time, at that – before one Middlesex bowler or another would find a fatal chink in these particular tail-enders. Warner says that he had not forgotten Bradford. Very wise, too; nor have we; but these good folk were not Wilson and Waddington, not by very long chalks. Gillie Reay hit all over the top of a straight ball from Hearne, and was bowled; and the final rearguard action was in the entirely amiable and good-humoured hands of Strudwick and Rushby. They played without the slightest sign of nerves, they took one or two here and one or two there, and once a ball from Stevens beat Murrell and scuttered off for four byes. But could anyone have really felt serious tension about the match result? Excitement, realization of hopes, triumph, yes; coupled with a natural anxiety to get the necessary preliminary (the last wicket) over and done with. At Bradford there had been scarifying doubt whether they could do it; here there could surely have been none. The only question was when; and at twenty past six Greville Stevens solved it. He tested Strudwick with a last prime googly, and it beat and bowled him; and Middlesex had won the match by 55 runs and the Championship by 2.39 points.

The entire population of Lord's went up like an explosion; the accumulated roar of delight must have been heard at Baker Street. From every conceivable direction the whole multitudinous mob poured excitedly over the barriers, a high proportion of the twenty thousand spectators emptied themselves out of the seats and the stands on to the wide green grass. The players scattered for the Pavilion; Warner, bending to secure the ball, was tackled smartly above the ankles and hoisted on high. Laughing, cheering, shouting, weeping, waving, vociferating, they bore him in this his greatest and most poignant moment to the Pavilion which was the centre of his life and imagination; and with this last spectacular gesture of affection and congratulation and farewell lowered him into the Long Room to meet the overwhelming pleasure and praises of his friends.

Then they stood on the grass and yelled until he came out on to the balcony to speak to them. What he could say could in nature be a mere fragmentary token of what he felt; and hardly anything of what he said could be heard by more than a very few. It would not be difficult to make up a speech for him, however difficult it would be for one in his place and situation to speak it unmoved; so let us all make up our own speech and assume that he did it justice. In his moment of great triumph and happiness he forgot nobody who had helped him to achieve it; and his friends the Middlesex

amateurs, and his generous vanquished opponent Percy
Fender, were there on the balcony to share his pleasure with
him. The closely-observed protocol of that day made it
necessary for Messrs Hendren, Hearne, Lee, Murrell and
Durston, who had also contributed modestly towards the
happiness of this occasion, to celebrate it a hundred yards away
in their rabbit-hutch, to which the fair-minded crowd, to its
everlasting credit, instantly repaired and not only demanded
but extracted a speech from Patsy Hendren. I cannot think
that Plum Warner can have felt this iniquitous separation to
be an acceptable feature of the rejoicings, or could ever have
done other than deplore that the admiration and gratitude
that he felt for the professionals in private could not have been
there and then, at the height of his triumph, expressed in
public. This was a defeat of the time, not of the man; the
ridiculous anomaly has of course been very properly done
away with years ago.

The newspapers showered him with congratulation and
cliché; the whole match became a nine days' wonder. Telegrams, messages, letters, flooded in upon him for days; he
printed a generous selection in his book. All sorts of people,
high and low, rich and poor, known and unknown, cricketers
and non-cricketers, Douglas and Hobbs and Fender, Charles
Fry and a number of Dukes and Earls, George Hirst and
Wilfred Rhodes, a handful of headmasters and bishops,
respectful N.C.O.'s from his Army days, actors and brigadiers
and limited companies and H.H. the Jam Sahib of Nawanagar
– all sent their messages of joy and goodwill. Even Lancashire,
wiping away tears of anger and frustration and mopping up
spilt champagne off the floor of Old Trafford, came generously
up to scratch. And no one's heartfelt message, and there were
literally thousands of them, was happier or more appropriate
than A. J. Webbe's, his first captain – A. J. Webbe, whose
courtesy and consideration for him when he was an untried
boy playing his first match for Middlesex so many years

before had helped to determine his own gentle and generous attitude to those under him, and no doubt in due time to influence theirs as well. The continuity had been preserved; and Warner in his unbelievable moment of success passed it on to those who should come after him. And he passed on, too, the memory of a great and hard-fought game to stand as the culmination of a great and hard-fought season which set the happy crown on a great and hard-fought career. Not many dedicated cricketers have been as fortunate as that.

Score:

MIDDLESEX

C. H. L. Skeet c Ducat b Rushby	2	c Fender b Hitch	106
H. W. Lee c Hitch b Fender	12	b Hitch	108
J. W. Hearne c and b Hitch	15	lbw b Rushby	26
E. Hendren b Reay	41	c Sandham b Rushby	5
P. F. Warner b Rushby	79	not out	14
F. T. Mann c and b Fender	12	c Peach b Fender	22
N. Haig b Reay	18	b Rushby	1
G. T. S. Stevens b Fender	53	not out	21
H. K. Longman b Fender	0		
H. R. Murrell c Ducat b Hitch	9	b Reay	0
F. J. Durston not out	0		
B 12 lb 12 nb 3	27	B 8 lb 4 w 1	13
	268	(7 wkts dec)	316

	O	M	R	W	O	M	R	W
Hitch	32.1	10	66	2	20	5	71	2
Rushby	23	9	48	2	22	7	73	3
Fender	28	4	76	4	16.5	2	70	1
Reay	26	17	31	2	18	1	61	1
Ducat	3	1	10	0	3	0	12	0
Shepherd	6	3	10	0	4	0	14	0

SURREY

J. B. Hobbs c Mann b Hearne	24	c Lee b Haig	10
A. Sandham not out	167	c and b Hearne	68
M. Howell c Murrell b Durston	7	st Murrell b Stevens	25
T. F. Shepherd c Murrell b Durston	0	c Hendren b Stevens	26

H. A. Peach hit wkt b Stevens				18	b Stevens			11
A. Ducat st Murrell b Lee				49	lbw b Hearne			7
P. G. H. Fender c Haig b Durston				30	b Durston			1
J. W. Hitch b Durston				1	b Stevens			6
G. M. Reay c Haig b Lee				6	b Hearne			5
H. Strudwick b Hearne				9	b Stevens			10
T. Rushby not out				6	not out			7
B 17 lb 5 nb 2				24	B 11 lb 1			12

(9 wkts dec)			341				188

	O	M	R	W	O	M	R	W
Durston	30	9	97	4	14	1	42	1
Haig	10	4	25	0	8	0	19	1
Stevens	16	0	72	1	13.4	0	61	5
Hearne	24	8	57	2	11	0	37	3
Lee	15	2	66	2	4	0	17	0

Middlesex won by 55 runs

7)   *The End*

SLOWLY the chattering crowds trickled away out of the gates; the milling, jostling enthusiasts in the Pavilion bars and corridors thinned out and departed, the fierce joyful emotional dressing-room excitements steadied and quietened at last. The scoreboard figures clicked back to zero, the attendants moved among paper-strewn benches, nothing was left to stare at the sky but the bare worn wicket and the green outfield now lightly damped with late August dew. Except in memory the classic match existed no longer, the slate was wiped clean. The lights came on in the Long Room; I doubt if the Pavilion emptied early that evening, for excitement and its warm reactions ran too high. I hope Plum Warner slept sound, though there is a high possibility that he could not sleep at all; the overwhelming culmination of his ambition and his life must have set taxing problems to his already over-driven emotional system. He must have lived that night, and perhaps for some time to come, in a heady and exhilarating daze.

The lights at Lord's came on, went out in due time. Night fell, was replaced by new day, the sequence asserted itself unsurprisingly. The great crisis and the great success receded; the newspapers, the letters, the encounters with friends, all renewed it, each time a little less brightly and immediately, but the elation stayed alive. The cricketers dispersed, some into the obscurity of the winter, some to Hastings or to Scarborough. Haig, Stevens, Mann, Hearne and Hendren were all at the Scarborough Festival in the next few days, and so were Percy Fender, Strudwick and Hitch. Jack Hobbs and Andrew Sandham contrived to be at both Scarborough and Hastings. Warner rested, put his feet up and relaxed, I very much hope, let the champagne froth and bubble evaporate, restored his equilibrium, lived quietly. The winning of the Championship had of course brought with it one pleasant additional bonus – he would now lead his side into the field once more, for Middlesex, Champion County, against the Rest of England at the Oval, by well-founded historic tradition (now in these late days unhappily abandoned) the last first-class match of the season with all the stars on show. This match took place a fortnight later; Middlesex fielded the same side as had beaten Surrey at Lord's; and the Rest fielded a fabulous collection of classic batsmen and bowlers whose joint and several reputations would have turned most opponents green with fright before the game started. The weather interfered and the match was drawn; the heat was off, the Middlesex bowlers were stale (and some of the Middlesex batsmen too) and the game resolved itself into a curious glorified Hit Parade of bravura performances by the great England batsmen. Middlesex started off by making 318 a little unevenly, Hendren being the only one of the leading batsmen to do himself justice. They were redeemed at the end of the order by an admirable stand between Stevens and Longman, who against some quite formidable bowling added 129 in just under two hours. I am particularly delighted to salute Longman's performance here; odd man out in the great Lord's game, with nothing but loyalty and keenness to show as his contribution, he gave of his best at the Oval, and in my sight this match is justified for his innings of 66 alone. When Middlesex went into the field the next day it must be regretfully recorded that the Rest of England batsmen clubbed them into oblivion and danced gleefully upon their bones, making a little matter of 603 for 5 in five hours. Hobbs and Jack Russell put up 185 for the first wicket in an hour and a half, Ernest Tyldesley and Hobbs then adding the next 152 in an hour and a quarter. Hobbs made 215 in just over three hours, bringing his total number of runs scored since Lee caught him in the slips at Lord's to well over 500 (another sidelong comment on Warner's happy fortune on that particular occasion). Everybody who went in got over 50, except Percy Holmes, who made 44, and Wilfred Rhodes, who was not out 29. The bowlers were so maltreated that I do not like to quote their analyses. You may look for them in *Wisden*; and, while you are goggling amazedly at Hearne's, I would ask you to do the memory of that fine cricketer the honourable service of recalling that in the ten crucial Middlesex matches that I have just passed under review, he took no less than 67 wickets, and that flesh and blood by this time could be asked to do no more.

Middlesex in their second innings dealt competently enough with half-pressure bowling. Rain interfered, and at six o'clock the stumps were pulled up; the happiest feature of the ending being that Plum Warner was not out 19, retiring thus undefeated from both Lord's and the Oval. And he took agreeable pleasure in the fact that whereas at Lord's he had walked off with Stevens, his youngest colleague, he now walked off at the Oval with Frank Mann, his successor as Captain, who had signalized his future intentions a moment or two before the end by depositing a ball from Frank Woolley on to the tramlines in the Harleyford Road.

> *Here were an end, had anything an end. . . .*
> *So did this old tale fade from memory,*
> *Till after, in the fulness of the days,*

I needs must find an ember yet unquenched,
And, breathing, blow the spark to flame. It lives,
If precious be the soul of man to man.

Browning nearly has it pat. Perhaps not quite; he was
talking of tragedy and I am not, so where Browning in the
second line above wrote 'woe' I have presumed to substitute
'tale'. And did it fade from memory? Only partly, I think.
Many cricketers remember it vividly still; yet going about
among them recently I have found quite a number to whom
this astonishing story is not so utterly familiar as to make the
re-telling of it a waste of time or an imposition on patience.

The summer of 1920 went down into winter, re-discovered
itself as usual in the spring and began all over again. A team
went cheerfully to Australia (Plum had helped to choose it at
the very beginning of the great sequence just reviewed, you
may remember) and took with it a number of old friends,
Hendren and Hearne among them, who were thus unhappily
prevented from enjoying certain grand celebrations at the
Café Royal in October when the Championship winners were
dined and wined by the Middlesex County Cricket Club.
Lee was absent from this festivity, too, as he was on his way
to coach in South Africa. Let us hope that absent friends were
toasted with a will, and that it did them good. The team that
went so cheerfully to Australia got the world's worst hammer-
ing, as everybody knows, and the England side (or sides) that
faced the returning Australians in the next baleful summer did
not do very much better. Jack Hearne fell ill on the tour and
played only once in the series next summer; Hendren did
moderately well in Australia, but failed rather conspicuously
when he got back home – the immediate aftermath of this
great story is twilit with anti-climax. Both rehabilitated
themselves, of course, Hendren in particular prolonging into
an evergreen maturity his wonderful ebullient talent and charm,
Hearne weathering illness and accident with resilience and a

loyal reliability that made him an indispensable feature of the cricket scene for years. Harry Lee, a step or two lower in proficiency but none in consistent assiduity, flourished far into the thirties with the rest. So in their differing fashions did Frank Mann and Nigel Haig, sterling and popular cricketers who became in their turns sterling and popular captains. Joe Murrell and Jack Durston both gave conspicuous service for many seasons before bowing themselves out. The boy prodigy Stevens, who in many ways must be accounted the most interesting of all Plum's performers, coming into the thick of the toughest of campaigns with the slenderest of experience and proving in the crisis of the conflict as decisive an influence as any of them, had a more spasmodic though perhaps a more remarkable career than any of these but the two great professionals. He was to play, on and off, for Middlesex for upwards of ten years; but he never had the time to spare for a full season of first-class cricket, and it is possible that this extraneous fact prevented him from being classed in cricket history as one of the great, and not just one of the very good, all-rounders. At all three departments he proved himself a player of lively and dependable verve; he went on two tours, he played in ten Tests, he was one of the immortal eleven who snatched the Ashes from Australia at the Oval in 1926 – and his versatility covered the engaging extremes of experience, from making 149 against the Australians' full Test side to dropping five catches before lunch in a Gents. v. Players' match, one off Jack Hobbs and three in successive balls off Wilfred Rhodes. One of the greatest spare-time players in English cricket, he nevertheless perhaps never quite reached the heights that his mentors and admirers predicted – which were limitless. It is no criticism of his decision to remain in a sense uncommitted, to say that he stands in the memory as a cricketer of style and character rather than, as he might have been, a figure of command.

These were Warner's principal helpers in this great last

season; and I list them to show what a team of talents, and
enduring talents at that, was gathered round him. Himself
apart, this same body of cricketers could be found active and
effective with very few changes for the best part of the next
decade. In the very next season, indeed, they won the
Championship again, as belatedly as in 1920, snatching it at
the last moment from Surrey as they had in our own treasured
record snatched it from Lancashire. Plum Warner, revisiting
Lord's, as he did so often that it must have seemed more like
coming home than going out for the day, must for very
many seasons have felt himself back in 1920, as Hendren and
Hearne piled up the runs or Haig ran soundlessly in along
his familiar curving track. The pride he must have felt in
this formidable and apparently unfading combination was the
greatest recompense for the necessary loss of his own powers
and the deprivation of his own capacity to share his companions' endeavours, and failures, and successes, as once he
could and did. He could recommend, advise, encourage; he
could be with them behind the scenes, behind the barrier.
But always now behind the barrier; he could not step over it
with them any more. There could be no compensation for that.

R. C. Robertson-Glasgow, that unusual cricketer-journalist
whose writing sometimes showed sudden glimpses of great
perceptive brilliance, first encountered Plum at the very outset
of this great season. 'Here he was in the flesh', he recorded,
'bald as an ostrich-egg under his Harlequin cap, slight, small-
boned, pale of face, and with nothing but cricket in his
conversation.' This may stand as the most adequate possible
sketch of him from a stranger's view – it says everything about
his appearance and habit, nothing about his nature (it did not
design to). But just as cricket shouldered everything else from
his talk, so in large measure it shouldered all other interests
from his life. His memoirs hint at an uncommon fascination
with naval and military history and a sterling if conventional
set of patriotic political views, but at little else in his long and

spacious life; so that when he no longer found the stamina to go on playing, nobody can be surprised that he devoted himself entirely to the game as an administrator and chronicler.

He had hardly got his breath back after his last match before he was writing accounts of it. He was already a practised and prolific cricket writer; his straightforward agreeable style had no especial distinction save that it clearly and adequately conveyed commitment and integrity, but he is a great deal more readable to this day than most of the contemporary reporters, whose manipulation of what I suppose may by courtesy be called the English language is in the last degree inept. Warner clearly enjoyed writing about cricket, and he gave himself from 1921 onwards full opportunities for indulging this addiction, as he proceeded then and there to found and edit the illustrious publication called *The Cricketer*, which for many years remained (*Wisden* of course excepted) the only considerable periodical concerned with the game, and with which he continued to be closely associated until the very end of his life. It has had its vicissitudes, and its appearance now is considerably changed from the close-printed green-covered magazine which I so eagerly devoured week by week all but half a century ago; but as a packed excitement-ridden consignment of fascinating gossip, commentary, history and statistics it was a recurring birthday present every week. The sheer word-bulk produced by the Editor himself in each number was prodigious – or would be considered so in anyone else – his knowledge of the game and its history and its personalities was so exact and encyclopaedic that the greatest trouble to him must have been writer's cramp rather than any disturbing problems about what material to use. The early years carried characteristic naïvetés; to an objective latter-day eye there is a devil of a lot about country-house cricket, and bewilderingly numerous paragraphs about cricketers and cricket matches whose sole aim to inclusion is that they were military or naval in origin, and there are bushels of photographs of regimental

elevens, country-house festival teams, Oxford University
Authentics, Free Foresters, I Zingari and the like. But I do not
wish to convey a false impression; first-class cricket was
admirably and minutely covered, the photographs were of
enduring value, and the scores of all sorts of games, first-class,
second-class, school and club alike, were more detailed than
anything but *Wisden*, and wider in scope even than that. For
many years cricket enthusiasts who saw nothing of Plum's
work behind the scenes in the administration of the game were
aware of his personality active in narration in the newspapers,
on the radio – he was one of the first B.B.C. commentators
on the game – and in *The Cricketer* each week. And every now
and then he produced a book, in which his slightly over-fluent,
almost facile journalist's manner was curbed and regulated by
what can only be called scholarship. He continued for the rest
of his active career to stimulate in thousands who could never
have known or seen him a deep and lively interest in cricket
on the pattern of his own.

This is not a biography of Plum Warner, though a full-
length study of his life in cricket might make a narrative as
fascinating to the student of social history and the psychology
of the privileged classes as to the cricket-watcher and the
objective student of the game. I am not going to attempt to
evaluate his influence on the first-class scene in the years of his
retirement from active play, although it was as powerful in
its own kind as that of any of the classic administrators of the
last hundred years, from Lord Harris, one of Plum's mentors,
to G. O. Allen, one of his Middlesex protégés. Gifted with
years and charm and authority, he exercised all these according
to his standards in the service of cricket, as player, writer,
selector, chairman, tour manager, secretary, organizer and
benevolent dictator for far longer than casual observers of his
frail frame could ever have thought possible. He had the
limitations that might have been expected of one of his
upbringing and tradition, and he had in the fullest measure

the corresponding virtues. In particular, he had an eye for promise in the young, and when he saw it he would go out of his way to foster it. The fatherly hand that he extended to Greville Stevens in 1919 was held out in turn to countless successors of that aspiring virtuoso as it had already in years long gone been held out to his forerunners. Names like Allen, Peebles, Robins, Edrich, Compton, Robertson, and no doubt the list runs on beyond as far as Titmus at least and maybe further, represent youths of keenness and promise who owed more than they could know or say to Warner's interest and encouragement, and he did not confine his fatherly ministrations to his own County. The young Walter Hammond, stricken almost to death with a tropical infection on a West Indies tour and despairing in a Bristol nursing home of ever regaining the vigour and promise that had raised high hopes in England and in himself, put it on record later that Warner's visit to him, a by no means famous or established player but simply a sick depressed young man lonely and dispirited, did as much as any medical treatment to put heart back into him. The moody withdrawn genius responded at once to the other's uncomplicated friendliness and sympathy. Hammond in later years may have been subject to the temperamental waywardnesses attendant upon the lonely and high-gifted; but he never forgot that kindness, so typical of him who offered it.

Weathering his customary physical set-backs, tirelessly and energetically active about the background of the game whose conduct he felt himself charged with, Plum Warner voyaged happily, by way of a knighthood, towards the verge of old age. During the Second World War he was virtually in charge at Lord's, being Deputy Secretary of the MCC for the duration and keeping the game most hearteningly alive there in those deadliest of days; he became President of the MCC in 1950 (and, I am prepared to bet, knew more about cricket than anyone ever appointed to that highest of cricketing offices before or since, and there have been very highly experienced players in that Chair) – and not long before his death he became the first Life Vice-President of the Club. He had so identified himself with Lord's that although he is by no means the greatest cricketer associated with the ground his is the name that most readily comes to mind as a kind of tutelary deity of that place; and it was altogether right that when a new stand was built between the Pavilion and the Grand Stand in 1958 it should be named the Warner Stand, and that after his death his ashes should be scattered on the turf immediately in front of it. As you come up the stairs at the back of this imposing building, his bronze bust stares you out of countenance – a little emaciated, perhaps, with a touch of minatory ferocity in it foreign to the essential gentleness of his temperament; but he presides there watchfully, as he seemed to do in life, and it does our unregenerate age no harm to be reminded of his benevolent if authoritarian presence.

The great cricket match that rounded off this great season, that was not only its culmination but the crown on Warner's own personal career, happened fifty years ago, and we have every excuse for having forgotten it. After all, like any other cricket match, all the cricket matches Warner or anyone else ever played in, it was over and done with before the bails off Strudwick's wicket, falling before Greville Stevens' last triumphant googly, had hit the ground. Over and done with and the pitch deserted, the score-boards unwound to nought, the slate wiped clean. A casual pastime, twenty-two men fooling around with bats and balls as any gang of youths may do for half an hour on any common. Why this fuss?

It is difficult to answer this one. No monuments are raised by cricketers, they create nothing, what they do flourishes momentarily and then fades. But then the same can be said of dancers, actors, musicians, they describe beautiful patterns of movement and sound but none of it leaves anything lasting behind it, only the memory.

The memory is the key, surely. The memory of Nijinsky

and Nureyev, of Chaliapin and Callas, of Irving and Olivier, is kept alive (setting aside recording processes on tape and film, which add a dimension but do not change the principle, I think) in the responsive memories of those whose imaginations the live performance fired. And disregarding the massive aesthetic problems here implied, and concentrating on this cricket match, it is in the memories and imaginations of those who played in it, or watched it, or heard about it, or read about it, that it still has the power to stir sympathies, tensions, fears, admirations, recriminations, and reminiscent delight. It does that partly because it is a cricket match and can be appreciated for its own sake as a very remarkable example in its kind; but it does it too because it symbolizes in a curious way a complex of emotions and satisfactions experienced by the central figure in it, that none of us can begin to share at all fully until we have put ourselves, as far as we can, in his peculiar place at that peculiar time. And that is precisely what I have tried to do. This match became a memory, as all other cricket matches can. But it became a memory with a meaning that nothing else has; it symbolizes the entirely happy and unexpected reward at the end of a courageous and difficult journey, in which the reward was not only the hero's but was bestowed also on all those of his companions and friends whose fascinating skills went to the necessary corporate endeavour.

It was his own personal experience more than it could ever be ours; but he helped to make it ours too, for he wrote the first authentic account of it, in his book *My Cricketing Life*, and everyone attempting to tell it all over again has naturally to use this. (I wish it had been fuller; in many ways I wish it had been better; but let that pass.) But the match became a classic because it was deeply bitten into so many people's imaginative memories – I hope I have been able to show why. It was living, and I am quite sure was frequently re-surveyed, in Plum's own memory, for as many as forty-three years.

And not only in his; for it is notable, as we look down the score sheet of that last memorable match, that participation in it, which should normally through the complicated nervous pressures engendered have been expected to shorten the lives of everyone involved, appears to have conferred longevity on the players, almost to a man. The match was played in the first year of the nineteen-twenties, between players of average age for a first-class match, many of whom had played before the First World War; it is surprising to find that all but four of the entire company survived into the nineteen-sixties. The first of these four, the handsome and athletic Ducat, went untimely at fifty-six, but he departed in full vigour with a melancholy appropriateness in the middle of an innings at Lord's, sinking to the ground while batting in a wartime match, within a few feet of where we have, as it were, just been watching him perform in the classic contest twenty-two years before. Apart from him only Tom Shepherd and Greville Stevens failed of all this party to reach three-score and ten; there were whole clusters of seventies, and a ripe handful of eighties, including Jack Hobbs and Plum himself; and Strudwick died only a few months ago aged ninety. Indeed the gods have been favourable. The memory of this great game was carried collectively forward for an impressive aggregate of years.

It is carried on still in the minds of the five who still happily survive and can, if they wish, check this account of it against first-hand impressions. Percy Fender's alert and penetrating shrewdness can still, no doubt, theorize cogently upon where Surrey went wrong, yet I am certain that he would still uphold with approval his fifty-year-old decision to go for the runs. The compact and fleet-footed Miles Howell is still with us, and so is the perennial Andy Sandham, whose amused watchful eyes absorbed so much on the cricket fields of the twenties and thirties and who gave and still gives so much of his equable and companionable personality to the game.

He and the other two of the match's century-makers have

now had half a century to remember their success in. Sand-ham's reminiscent pleasure must be leavened with an ironic regret; Skeet and Lee, on the other hand, must harbour recollections wholly unalloyed, the lovely rosy afterglow of complete and joyful success. Skeet, who spent his career in distant parts and never, I believe, made any other first-class hundred, must see this golden hour of his as a tiny jewel of delight glimpsed over limitless intervening chasms of alien experience; Harry Lee, professional to the bone, remembers it surely but rather as a good job of work well accomplished than as a romantic symbol – a job which he was to repeat in other circumstances, and with other stresses and pressures to combat, many times in the years ahead. Venturing, like Sandham, into his eighties in this jubilee year, he lives near Lord's and attends the cricket frequently, no doubt sternly critical of his juniors and, I hope, happily reminiscent of his own days and especially of those chronicled here.

As for Greville Stevens, who was six years younger than anyone else in the game, he is but lately dead; he retained, as might be expected, to the verge of his seventies, the native zestful wit and style which while he was still a boy at school so powerfully reinforced his enormous talent. He did not forget this match, he lately rekindled the feel of it in the minds of devotees by his published recollections of it: 'everything was marvellous to me', he said of the final scenes of acclamation, 'because I had never witnessed a scene like that before' – and the sense of youthful wonder and excitement survived refresh-ingly in him after fifty years. It was a happy pattern of events that allowed it to turn out that the youngest member of the conquering eleven, in whom Plum took such a special and personal pride, should be the one to celebrate the jubilee by publicly expressing his own special and personal pride in Plum. 'Under Plum we all tried beyond our limitations', he said . . . 'without him we would never have gained the day.' It was a day that, in however modest a fashion, coloured and lightened the lives of those who shared it for half a century. We all have our good days; this was theirs, and it was an especially good one.

Plum Warner grew old before his friends' eyes, diligent in attendance at Lord's as always, shrinking diminutively into the bowed spare bright-eyed figure which is all that most of us remember of his physical person. One of the telegrams flooding in on the morning after the great day had contained a specific wish – 'May you at least live to 79, your score, to help govern the game you have long so adorned'. In the upshot 79 was peanuts; Plum failed by only a few months to reach ninety, and he moved steadily and firmly about his familiar Pavilion until a very short time before the end. He was an accepted institution, but he was a warmly beloved personality as well; and long after he could concern himself really actively or intimately in the affairs of the great game he would seem wherever he passed to attract a kind of unspoken respect, not only for his age or his authority or his achievements, but also for the undimmed dedication of his character, which time and age never altered.

Old men live much in the past and there can be no doubt that he studied his memories more closely than most, and plenty of them there must have been. I have seen him myself standing alone looking out upon Lord's, pensively; who can say what match or matches he was seeing, whether the one going on in front of him or a chance incident in any one of the thousands, literally thousands, that he had played in or watched or heard about in the unending sequence of his years? Nothing is more certain than his consistent pleasure in old friends, old incidents, old experiences; they revived for him the active companionship and common purpose on the field that had been the central experience of his life and for which no amount of reporting or administering could be a real substitute. Greville Stevens it was again who supplied a vivid and illuminating picture which records so little and yet tells so much: 'Plum in old age', he told me, 'always held my hand in his little two hands and said, "You bowled many fine balls for Middlesex, Sir".' I find the gesture, the strange courtliness, the touching deference of one who was once the master to one who was once his pupil, the almost ritualistic manner of the utterance – I find all of these disproportionately moving. It is more than a cry from Age to Youth; it is a loving and cherishing recall of something in the past that meant much to the two of them together, the memory of which was of common enterprise and endeavour enriching both lives. It tells me a little about both men.

I myself have a tiny memory of Plum Warner, to which I have no right, as it is merely of something I overheard him say. This was perhaps the last time I ever saw him at Lord's, a year or two before his death, not more; and I happened to pass him where he stood in conversation with a friend, to whom as I came level I heard him say, 'You will give my love to that young man, won't you?' That is all, and it was none of my business, but the sentence stuck in my mind because I felt it to be completely characteristic of the man who had uttered it. For he spent his life encouraging young men into the disciplines and the delights that he himself had submitted and responded to for the whole of his privileged but single-minded maturity; and as everyone who knew him always testifies, with his encouragement came his love, calling out in the recipient a corresponding affection in its turn. It was his pleasure, and in his own estimation his duty, to pass on for the sake of the game he loved so well the benefit of his experience and his dedication for those who would follow and pass it on in their own time; and that is why it is such a pleasure, and a kind of duty beside, to pass on in the jubilee year of celebration, for the delight of cricket-lovers all over the world, the tale of a success which hardly anyone foresaw and which nobody on earth has ever grudged.